HEROES AND WARRIORS

Crazy Horse

SACRED WARRIOR OF THE SIOUX

JASON HOOK
Plates by RICHARD HOOK

Firebird Books

Acknowledgements

Thanks from the author to Ian M. West. Also to Marty Miller at the Nebraska State Historical Society for her help and advice with photographs; and to all the other individuals and institutions who also assisted in providing references and illustrations.

First published in the UK 1989 by Firebird Books
P.O. Box 327, Poole, Dorset BH15 2RG

Copyright © 1989 Firebird Books Ltd
Text copyright © 1989 Jason Hook

Distributed in the United States by
Sterling Publishing Co, Inc,
387 Park Avenue South, New York, NY 10016–8810

Distributed in Australia by
Capricorn Link (Australia) Pty Ltd
PO Box 665, Lane Cove, NSW 2066

British Library Cataloguing in Publication Data

Hook, Jason
    Crazy Horse: sacred warrior of the
    Sioux. ——— (Heroes and Warriors).
    1. Sioux. Chiefs. Crazy Horse, 1842 ?–1877
    I. Title II. Series
    970.004'97

ISBN 1 85314 013 9 (paperback)
ISBN 1 85314 025 2 (cased)

Series editor Stuart Booth
Designed by Kathryn S.A. Booth
Typeset by Inforum Typesetting, Portsmouth
Monochrome origination by Castle Graphics, Frome
Colour separations by Kingfisher Facsimile
Colour printed by Barwell Colour Print (Midsomer Norton)
Printed and bound in Great Britain at The Bath Press

Crazy Horse

SACRED WARRIOR OF THE SIOUX

CRAZY HORSE TERRITORY

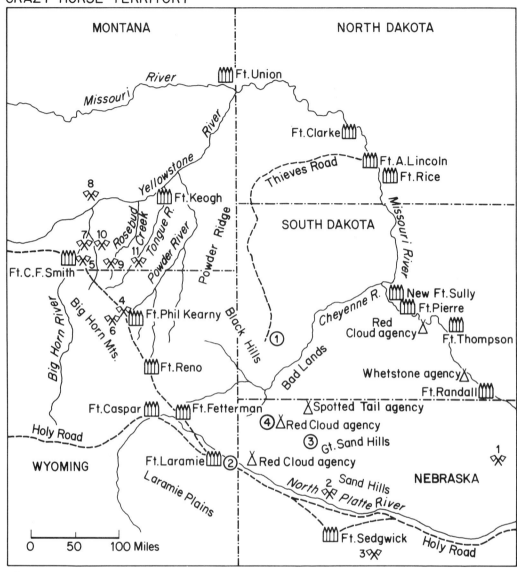

① Crazy Horse – Curly-born, Rapid Creek, 1841

② Great Lakota Council, 1857

③ Curly named Crazy Horse

④ Crazy Horse fatally wounded, 1877

Battles ⚔

1 Curly kills Omaha woman	7 He Dog and Crazy Horse raid Crow, 1870
2 Bluewater, 1855	8 Fight with Custer and Stanley's troops 1873
3 Sumner's attack, 1857	9 Rosebud Creek 1876
4 Fetterman Massacre, 1866	10 Little Big Horn 1876
5 Hayfield Fight, 1867	11 Miles' attack on Crazy Horse 1877
6 Wagon Box Fight, 1867	

One does not sell the earth upon which the people walk
(Crazy Horse 1875)

The Greatest Leader

European settlement of North America met with its fiercest adversary in the shape of the Lakota or Western (Teton) Sioux, the powerful Indian nation that dominated the heart of the Great Plains. Central in the Lakota resistance to the white man's invasion were the people of the Oglala Sioux. The heart of the stubborn defence of their homeland was Crazy Horse. A peerless warrior and revered mystic, Crazy Horse fought for the traditions of his people, until those same people wearied of war and, in some cases, turned against him.

The Plains culture region.

Dr V.T. McGillycuddy, assistant post surgeon at Fort Robinson where Crazy Horse died, said of the ill-fated Oglala leader:

In him everything was made a second to patriotism and love of his people. Modest, fearless, a mystic, a believer in destiny, and much of a recluse, he was held in veneration and admiration by the younger warriors who would follow him anywhere . . . I could not but regard him as the greatest leader of his people in modern times.

The Sioux

Crazy Horse's people, known collectively as the Dakota nation, are popularly called the Sioux. Yet that word is a corruption, made by the early French settlers, of the name Nadouessioux. In turn, that was the Chippewa name for their 'adders' or 'enemies'. The Sioux nation had a complex structure, with a large number of tribal divisions and their own names.

The Sioux peoples' own name for themselves is Ocheti Shakowin, the 'Seven Council Fires', or seven tribes that originally formed their nation: the Mdewakanton, Wahpeton, Wahpekute, Sisseton, Yankton, Yanktonai and Teton. In time, these groups became separated by dialect and geography into three distinct historical divisions.

The easternmost group, comprising the first four of the council fires, became the Dakota or Santee Sioux, retaining their agricultural tradition between the forks of the Missouri and Mississippi. By 1770, the second division, the Nakota, including and collectively referred to as the Yankton and Yanktonai, were living between the Missouri and James Rivers.

The Lakota or Teton Sioux, the westernmost spark from the council fires, were Crazy Horse's people. Just as their original nation comprised the seven fires, so the Lakota became divided into seven sub-tribes as they migrated in the 1700s from the Mississippi across the Missouri to the Great Plains. The Oglala (Those Who Scatter Their Own) and Brulé (Burnt Thighs) were the first Lakota west of the Missouri. They were followed by the Miniconjou (Those Who Plant By The Stream); Sans Arcs (Without Bows); Oohenonpa (Two Kettles); Sihasapa (Blackfoot) and Hunkpapa (Those Who Camp By The Entrance). Ideally, these seven tribes united each summer to renew the nation's unity; but in practice, each tribe was autonomous.

Crazy Horse was a member of the Hunkpatila band, one of seven bands that in theory made up the Oglala tribe. In reality, the name, number and size of the Oglala hunting bands fluctuated according to the prominence of different chiefs.

As early as the 1500s, the Sioux were established east of the Mississippi headwaters. There are historic records of their living in the Milles Lacs region of Minnesota in 1650, where they demonstrated a Woodlands culture. They hunted, raised corn and foraged for wild rice in the woodlands, travelling the lakes and rivers in bark canoes, and defending their lands aggressively. The formation of the Hudson's Bay trading company in 1670 made firearms available to the traditional eastern enemies of the Sioux, the Chippewa, through trade with their Indian allies. Hardpressed by the well-armed Chippewa and drawn by the rich buffalo herds that roamed the Great Plains, the Sioux migrated westward. This migration caused the division into Lakota, Nakota and Dakota, as the three groups settled into new territories, and led to the Lakotas' adoption of a Plains culture.

In 1680, Father Louis Hennepin identified some Sioux west of the Mississippi at the Sauk rapids. By 1700, French fur trader Pierre Charles le Sueur placed their territory on Blue Earth River, between the upper Mississippi and Missouri, with the westernmost vanguard hunting buffalo on the James River. In 1743, the La Vérendrye brothers placed the 'Prairie Sioux' fifty miles north of Pierre, South Dakota, on the eastern bank of the Missouri.

The acquisition of the horse, that came to dominate their culture, created a new boldness in the westward sweep of the Sioux after 1750. Their own calendar or 'winter count' records the discovery, in 1765, of Pa Sapa – the sacred Black Hills – that would become the beating heart of Lakota life and lands.

As the last major tribe on to the Plains, the Lakota had to fight for their new lands. In 1792, they defeated the Arikara tribe who were already

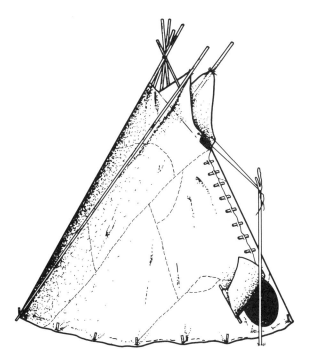

decimated by smallpox. By 1800, the Lakota had sufficient horses, warriors and spirit to possess the territory that they would defend against the white man. They claimed land south to the Platte River, east to the Missouri, north to the Yellowstone; and would dislodge tribes such as their greatest enemy, the Crow, west of the Black Hills to the Teton Mountains. The foremost of the Lakota tribes, the Brulé, lived in the White River, while the Oglala roamed west of the Bad River to Pa Sapa.

The Winter Count

The early history of the Sioux, aside from the accounts of the first trappers and traders, is recorded in their own historic calendars known as 'winter counts'. These pictographic records were painted on deerskins, often in spiral form, by the tribal historians. Each year was commemorated by its most significant event, and the winter counts were handed down through the generations.

The winter counts of White Man Stands in Sight of the Oglala, of Baptiste Good (Brown Hat) of the Brulé, and of Iron Shell of the Miniconjou record events as far back as the 1700s. A meteor shower made 1833 the Winter of Shooting Stars, while 1850 was the Winter of Smallpox and notated by a picture of a spotted face.

Pictographs were also made to narrate important events such as battles. The pictographic record of the Oglala historian Amos Bad Heart Bull illustrates many of the important events in the life of his cousin, Crazy Horse. The Lakota used to say: 'A people without history is like wind on the buffalo grass.'

The tipi or lodge was a tilted cone of three or four main poles interspersed with a number of strengthening poles, with a dressed buffalo skin cover. It could be dismantled very rapidly by two experienced women, and hauled by two or three horses. The tipi was equipped with smoke-flaps, permitting an interior fire, and a draught-excluding liner. It was warm and waterproof in the winter, and stream-lined and sturdy enough to resist the strongest winds. In summer, its sides could be rolled up for ventilation.

The Land and the People

The buffalo was the Lakota's staff of life, yielding food, shelter, clothing, fuel and numerous utensils. Thronging the Great Plains in vast numbers, these short-sighted, keen-scented beasts made a fearsome prey, whose capture was a spectacular, dangerous undertaking. The extinction of the buffalo at the white man's hands was one of the most important factors in the extinction of the Plains Indians' way of life.

The Great Plains of North America are a vast grassland covering some million square miles between the Mississippi and the Rockies, from Canada down to Texas. Limitless horizons are punctuated by occasional ranges of hills and cottonwood valleys, surrounding rivers that become mere dusty veins in summer. Constant winds sway deep-rooted 'buffalo-grass', forage for buffalo whose vast numbers once blackened the Plains.

The nineteenth century homeland of the Oglala spread outward from the Black Hills, to where now lie the states of Wyoming, Montana, South Dakota and Nebraska. Westward loomed the foreboding shadow of the Rockies; northwards lay a wasteland of buttes and crags, the Badlands; to the east were the White River hunting grounds of the Brulé.

Migration of the Lakota into the Black Hills dislodged several tribes from the region. The Kiowa were driven to the southern Plains, homeland of the Comanche. The Crow, pushed north to Montana, became the Lakota's most implacable foe. The Cheyenne were also swept aside by the Lakota, but formed a permanent alliance with them in 1843, when the Lakota people recovered one of the Cheyenne's Sacred Arrows, an ancient medicine item stolen by the Pawnee. The Plains tribes also included the Blackfoot, Assiniboin and Arapaho, all sharing with the Lakota a common culture that revolved around the buffalo and horse.

Buffalo and Sacred Dog

Buffalo used to roam the Plains in such numbers that Pedro de Castañeda, Coronado's chronicler, could only compare them to the fish in the sea. In 1830, George Catlin, the great western painter, wrote:

the buffalo congregate into such masses in some places as literally to blacken the prairies for miles together. It is no uncommon thing . . . to see several thousands in a mass, eddying and wheeling about under a cloud of dust.

Not only were the buffalo plentiful, they also provided for every conceivable need of the Plains Indians. Every part of their meat was eaten, boiled in water carried to camp in a container fashioned from the buffalo's belly, over a fire stoked by the dung. Buffalo hide was fashioned into clothes and shelter – for lodges or tipis – tanned with an agent made from the brains and liver. Boiled buffalo hooves glued the head on to an arrow, fired by a bow string made from the sinew. Even the buffalo's tail made a fly-brush.

When the Lakota were still poor in horses, they relied upon wolf-skin disguises in order to hunt the buffalo, or drove the heavy beasts into snow drifts in the winter. Large amounts of meat were secured by the communal drive or *piskun*; there a holy man with power to call the buffalo lured them to a high cliff. The entire band then surrounded and stampeded the herd over the cliff. Arrow-heads still litter the floors of cliffs favoured by tribes for the *piskun*.

The arrival of horses in great numbers created the golden age of the Plains Indians. After 1600, Pueblo Indians working on Spanish ranches in Texas and New Mexico passed on their knowledge, with stray and stolen horses, to the southern Plains tribes. Horses gradually filtered north and by 1750 were fully integrated into the culture of the Lakota so that General George Crook could one day describe them as the greatest light cavalry the World had ever known.

The nineteenth-century Lakota, a mounted, nomadic people, demonstrated the culture which is now considered typical of their people. The hunt was transformed into a glorious cavalry charge, on specially trained mounts – 'buffalo-runners' – and more meat could be carried back to camp. The horse's exceptional utility led to its name 'sacred dog'. Larger

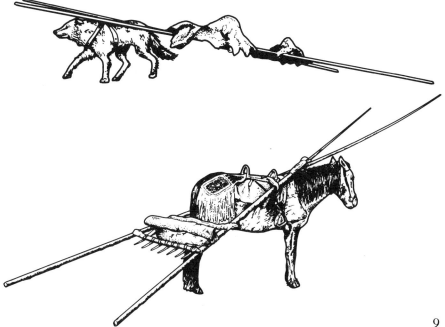

Before the arrival of the horse on the North American continent, the Indians used dogs to haul all their possessions and homes across the Plains on A-shaped frames called travois. The advent of the horse meant a great increase in material wealth for the Indians of the Plains. Longer lodge-poles could be hauled to fresh campsites, constructed into travois, so that the Indians' tipis became larger and their possessions more numerous.

9

Lakota eagle wingbone whistle, adorned with beaded ring, antelope skin, sweetgrass bundle, beaded thongs terminating in red-dyed skin bundles, and a rawhide necklace. Such whistles were blown by warriors during battle and when undertaking the Sun Dance ceremonies, to invoke the power of the eagle, messenger of the Sun.

lodges were now used, hauled along behind the horses in V-shaped travois.

The Lakota adopted a seasonal pattern which mirrored migrations and habits of the buffalo. From August (Moon of Ripe Plums) to November (Moon of Hairless Calves), the various hunting bands roamed independently, moving camp when buffalo were scarce. Meat and wild vegetables were stored for the winter, and new lodges made. Each band made its way gradually to its regular winter camp, often in a sheltered river valley. After December (Moon of Frost in the Tipi), camp was only moved when lack of resources so dictated.

When April (Moon of the Birth of Calves) brought the warm breath of spring, the Lakota began a new year. Leaving the winter sites in May (Moon of Thunderstorms), separate bands often camped together, as rich grazing drew the buffalo into larger herds. By July (Cherry Blackening Moon), all Oglala hunting bands would ideally be camped together, though a union of the entire Lakota tribe was rare. With many mouths to feed, warrior societies enforced hunting regulations in order to prevent individuals scaring away abundant herds. When the tribe was united, elders organised the greatest of the Lakota religious ceremonies, the Sun Dance. This complex ritual, the most striking aspect of which was the self-torture of supplicant dancers, renewed tribal unity and reaffirmed the People's relations with a world considered in all aspects to be sacred.

Before the arrival of the white man, the Lakota felt in control of, and in harmony with, an abundant world, bound only by the Earth below and the Sky above. The Oglala Luther Standing Bear recalled:

The old Lakota was wise. He knew that a man's heart away from nature becomes hard; he knew that lack of respect for growing, living things soon led to lack of respect for humans too. So he kept his youth close to its softening influence.

The Lakota's dispute with the white man was clearly not just a battle for land; it was a clash of cultures.

Warfare

Pipe tomahawks with pierced blade and brass tack decorations. The hatchet-type, shown here, was typical among the Lakota in the period 1860–80.

Of the Lakota, Francis Parkman, the great nineteenth-century historian, wrote:

War is the breath of their nostrils. Against most of the neighbouring tribes they cherish a rancorous hatred, transmitted from father to son, and inflamed by constant aggression and retaliation.

As newcomers to the Black Hills, the Lakota had to fight constantly to assert themselves. Ownership of Mother Earth was not conceived, but defending their hunting lands was a practical necessity. Survival was achieved through regular displays of aggression against the Crow, Pawnee and Shoshoni.

The importance of the horse was such that horse-raiding was the most popular form of war. Warriors made stealthy forays into the heart of enemy camps, stealing their finest ponies. Inevitably this led to bloody reprisal raids – not for horses but for scalps.

A warrior's record of his war deeds was vital to his standing in the tribe, and a system of exploits or 'coups' was recognised. The coup proper was to touch an enemy without harming him, so demonstrating superiority. Other coups, such as killing an enemy in hand-to-hand combat, were accorded varying credit. It is a measure of Lakota aggression that they rated the taking of a scalp more highly than most Plains tribes.

Both the tribe and the warrior fought constantly to assert themselves in a merciless world. A warrior recorded and displayed his coups in his costume and regalia, particularly through feather heraldry. Thus, the first man to strike an enemy boasted of his 'first coup' by wearing an eagle feather upright at the back of his head.

Warfare was a constant feature of Plains life; Indians slept with their weapons at their sides. Warriors vied with each other with shows of recklessness, and demonstrated a bravery emanating from a belief that death in battle was a glorious death.

Lakota war-bonnet with beaded brow-band. The double leather trailer of golden eagle tail feathers has cloth-wrapped stems and yellow horse-hair streamers; an eagle 'fluffy' is hung by a thong from the brow-band. The right to wear such magnificent bonnets, symbols of officership among the tribe and soldier societies, was earned only by the élite.

'Hairy Man From The East'

We did not think of the great open plains, the beautiful rolling hills, and winding streams with tangled growth, as 'wild'. Only to the white man was nature a 'wilderness', and only to him was the land 'infested' with 'wild' animals and savage people. To us it was tame. Earth was bountiful and we were surrounded with the blessings of the Great Mystery. Not until the hairy man from the east came and with brutal frenzy heaped injustices upon us and the families we loved was it 'wild' for us. When the very animals of the forest began fleeing from his approach, then it was that for us the 'Wild West' began.
(Luther Standing Bear)

After 1700, the migration of the Lakota was mirrored by the progress west of white trappers and traders. The French were the initial pathfinders, though they were supplanted by the English Hudson's Bay Company following the French and Indian Wars of 1754–63. Traders travelling the upper Missouri found the Sioux aggressive and with no desire to accumulate wealth, showing a lofty independence like 'the air they breathed or the wind that blew'.

By 1800, buffalo and Indian alike were being driven west of the

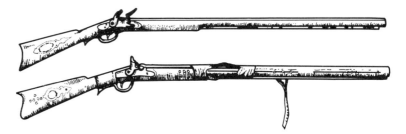

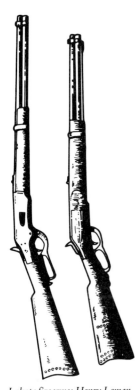

Lakota firearms: Henry Leman flintlock trade rifle and Leman percussion rifle with rawhide repairs and brass tack adornment, issued in government annuities 1850–70(top); Winchester Model 1866 carbine, a popular post-Civil War trade gun and Sitting Bull's Winchester Model 1866 carbine, surrendered in 1881(above); United States Springfield cavalry carbine, Model 1873, owned by Young Man Afraid of his Horses after its capture at the Little Bighorn, and a remarkable composite rifle, fashioned from an 1866 United States Army Model .50–70 barrel and receiver and .45–70 stock and lock, captured from the Lakota by Fort Robinson troops (opposite).

Mississippi by European settlement of north-east North America. The opening of the American West was founded by the Lewis and Clark expedition along the Missouri, and the subsequent settlement of hard-living white trappers, the mountain men. The American Fur Company, chartered in 1808, bidded against the Canadians for the Indian beaver trade with growing quantities of poor whiskey. The Lakota, who still travelled east to the Woodlands in spring, accepted the white man's guns, metal tools, tobacco, beads and cloth, and refrained from hostilities that might endanger their eastern relatives. The 1830 Indian Removal Act empowered President 'Sharp Knife' Jackson to drive the eastern tribes towards the hunting grounds of the Lakota.

Fort Pierre was built in the Dakotas in 1831 and three years later a crude stockade, Fort William, was built on the junction of the North Platte and Laramie Rivers. Later known as Fort Laramie, this stockade was constructed by William Sublette and Robert Campbell of the Rocky Mountain Fur Company, who invited Oglala chief Bull Bear to trade with them. Drawn by copious quantities of liquor and promises of fresh hunting grounds, the Oglala and Brulé migrated south. This brought them into close proximity with their bitter enemies, the Pawnee, and placed their camps directly in the path of what would become the Oregon Trail.

The wooden wheels of the first great wagon trains cut a swathe across the Plains in 1841. As the emigrants' axes chopped down the groves of trees, their cattle cropped the rich grasses, and their wagons scared the buffalo, the resentful Lakota demanded or exacted 'tributes'. However, at this time of crisis, the Oglala – already dismayed by whiskey – were cleft in two by tribal rivalries.

White traders had grown to favour a plump chief named Old Smoke, causing bitterness among the Bear people, aggressively led by Chief Bull Bear. Some years previously, Bull Bear had thrown down a challenge, by shooting Old Smoke's horse in the middle of that chief's camp circle. Old Smoke exacted his revenge in the fall of 1841, when Bull Bear rode into Smoke's camp on the Chugwater branch of Laramie fork. The Indians were drunk, and Bull Bear was shot dead; his assailant was rumoured to be an ambitious warrior of the Bad Face band, named Red Cloud. The killing created a split in the Oglala that was to pervade Crazy Horse's life.

12

The dead chief's Bear band drifted south-east between the Platte and Smoky Hill rivers, while the Bad Faces hunted north-west of the Platte to the Black Hills. By 1846, Old Smoke was chief of those Indians that persisted in begging idly at Fort Laramie, and disdainfully referred to by the free Oglala as the Loafers-Around-The-Fort. In 1841, as the Oglala unity was being shattered, Crazy Horse was born.

The Light-haired Boy

According to the testimony of his boyhood companion Chips, and of Dr McGillycuddy, Crazy Horse was born in the fall of 1841, the Winter of the Big Horse Steal. His birthplace was on Rapid Creek, east of the Black Hills, Pa Sapa. Before he earned his adult name, he was known as the Light-haired Boy, or just Curly. His father was called Crazy Horse, a humble but respected holy man of the Hunkpatila band of the Oglala. The Hunkpatila or 'End-of-Circle' band always camped at one point of the Oglala crescent when the tribe was together. Curly's mother was a Brulé, sister of Spotted Tail, who was now eighteen and killing a rival chief in his rise to prominence among his tribe. Curly's mother died when he was young, but her place in the lodge was taken by her younger

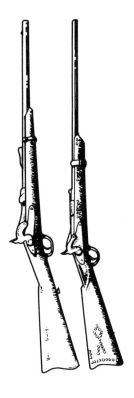

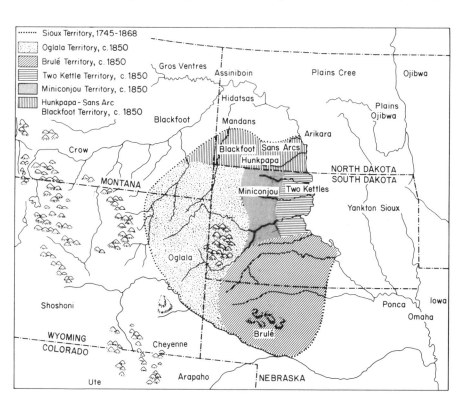

The homeland of the Lakota and Plains tribes in 1850.

13

Lakota umbilical cord protective amulets, of buckskin, bead-work and metal cones. Young children were called 'carry their navels', because they wore such amulets containing their own umbilical cords. The protection of the cord was considered, by extension, to grant sacred protection to the child. Thus amulets were fashioned after the protective symbols of the turtle (upper) which is difficult to kill, and the lizard (lower) which is difficult to catch.

sister. Curly had an older sister, and would have a younger brother who would take his uncle's name of Little Hawk.

Even as a child, Curly was set apart from other Lakota by his pale complexion and light wavy hair, characteristics that gave him his nickname and distinguished him throughout his life. Short Bull, an Oglala contemporary described Curly's adult appearance:

His hair was very light . . . he was a trifle under six feet tall. Crazy Horse had a very light complexion, much lighter than the other Indians. His features were not like the rest of us. His face was not broad and he had a sharp, high nose. He had black eyes that hardly ever looked straight at a man, but they didn't miss much that was going on all the same.

To the Lakota something unusual, such as an albino buffalo bull, was considered *wakan* or sacred. Curly, aware of his physical quirks, was a strangely quiet, thoughtful child; his father, a holy man, watched him with special interest.

When Curly was born, his umbilical cord was cut away and placed in a protective amulet fashioned after a turtle, to symbolise longevity. His ears were pierced during the first Sun Dance ceremony held after he could walk. Aged five, Curly received his own clothes and belongings to look after, and his umbilical amulet, and was known as a 'carry your navel' child. When the band moved camp, he rode on a horse travois.

Old Smoke, of the Loafers, liked whiskey, sugar and the 'black medicine', coffee; so Curly spent much of his early life around the trading posts on the Platte, where travellers on the Oregon Trail often mistook him for a captive white boy. Roaming north of the Platte, he learned the traditional ways of his people. When tall enough to ride, Curly received his first horse from his father, and by the age of ten had killed his first buffalo and held his seat on a wild horse. To celebrate these achievements, his father led Curly around the Hunkpatila camp calling that his son would now be called His Horse On Sight. The women of the camp, though, persisted in calling the light-haired boy Curly.

Though quieter than his comrades, Curly competed with the best of them in the rigorous training that prepared a Lakota youth for war. During the sham battles that they fought, Curly formed a special friendship with a comrade called High Back Bone or Hump. They were pledged to share their acquisitions and protect each other in battle, for High Back Bone was Curly's *kola* – his friend.

Horse Creek

'Since old Mahto-Tatonka (Bull Bear) died the People have been like children that do not know their own minds. They are no better than a body without a head.' So Eagle Feather spoke of the Oglala in 1846 to Francis Parkman. The old people were calling for peace, jealous of any threat to their supply of trade goods. The young warriors were buying their coffee in a different way, scaring the emigrants into parting with it, or stealing it from those foolish enough to wander off alone.

The stream of white-topped wagons had become a great river, and hostilities were increasing, when in the Moon of Making Fat, 15th June 1845, Colonel S. W. Kearney met the Oglala and Brulé at Laramie. He marched his five companies of dragoons up and down, fired his howitzers, and gave the Lakota beads and looking glasses, telling them that the travellers on the Oregon Trail were not to be harmed.

In 1849, the government bought and stationed troops at Fort Laramie. Further east at Grand Island, Fort Stephen Kearney was established. The Lakota and Cheyenne defiantly raised a war-party of five hundred warriors against the Pawnee, and raided the Fort Kearney supply train. Then, a new type of emigrant – 'forty-niners' bound for California to seek gold – thronged into their lands, bringing with them an epidemic of cholera. Curly's people fled north from the sickness, which left every lodge of one camp on the White River silently concealing its dead. One Cheyenne chief, Little Old Man, dressed for war and rode through his camp, singing: 'If I could see this thing; if I knew where it came from – then I would ride right into it and kill it.' Then he too fell with the stomach cramps.

The next year brought no relief, marked on the winter count of the Oglala as the Winter of Smallpox. Another 50,000 travellers passed Laramie that spring, and when the disease finally dissipated, the Indians were in an ugly mood. In response to pleas from alarmed agents and traders, the government sent messengers to the Plains tribes calling them to a great council at Laramie.

In July 1851, the Moon of Ripening Cherries, Curly's people joined a great gathering of Lakota and Cheyenne at Fort Laramie, there to meet Thomas 'Broken Hand' Fitzpatrick, Indian Agent on the Platte, and D.D. Mitchell, Superintendent of Indian Affairs. In September, the Moon of Yellow Leaves, the Shoshoni arrived; a Lakota warrior rushed out to kill their leader, Washakie, who had killed his father. Only the

Lakota dance shield of the Elk Dreamers Society. Constructed from painted muslin stretched over a willow hoop, it is decorated with a blue-painted elk head design, a sweetgrass bundle, hawk bells, orange-dyed horned-owl feathers and brown and white sage grouse tail-feathers. Lakota men who shared similar visions banded together in dreamer cults, each with distinctive songs, ceremony and regalia depicting their particular guardian spirit.

Oglala pipe and tobacco bag of tanned, white skin, decorated with typical Lakota beadwork, and quilled rawhide fringes. The smoking and giving of tobacco, with its associated utensils, were part of all major ceremonies.

physical intervention of a French interpreter saved the council from becoming a full-scale war.

The council moved thirty-six miles down the Platte to Horse Creek on 4th September, because the wagon-train of gifts promised to the Indians was late, and their ponies had cropped the grass. Two days later, 1,000 Lakota warriors singing their peace songs paraded before the commissioners and received gifts of tobacco. The next day, Curly stared wide-eyed as the Lakota feasted the Cheyenne, Arapaho and their enemies the Shoshoni; the pulse of the drum and shrill singing continuing until dawn.

On 8th September, a cannon's report opened the great Horse Creek council. Curly, aged ten, sat with the women and children behind the warriors, converged on the council lodge where the commissioners and the chiefs smoked the pipe. Then Mitchell outlined the purpose of the council. He said that the Great Father wished the Indians to stop molesting the emigrants and allow forts to be built on their lands. They should also refrain from attacking each other, and recognise boundaries to their lands. Each tribe was to select one chief to sign the treaty, and in return they would receive $50,000 of annuities for fifty years (reduced later by Congress to ten).

The Oglala held their eagle-wing fans to their faces when they heard these strange words. They did not understand this white man's ownership of Mother Earth that would prevent them from raiding for horses and prestige. When it came to selecting one chief for the entire Lakota nation, the chiefs shook their heads. Thus, Mitchell had to select his own 'paper chief', the Brulé Conquering Bear, who told Mitchell:

I am not afraid to die but to be chief of all the nation I must be a big chief, or in a few months I shall be dead on the prairie. I have a wife and children. I do not wish to leave. If I am not a powerful chief, my enemies will be on my trail all the time.

On 17th September, the various headmen 'touched the pen' to the treaty. The Oglala now called the Oregon Trail 'the Holy Road', for the treaty said that its people could not be touched. Conquering Bear, wearing the pantaloons and general's uniform presented to him, was the first chief to sign; but no Oglala or Cheyenne touched the pen:

You have split my land and I don't like it. These lands once belonged to the Kiowa and the Crow, but we whipped these nations out of them, and in this we did what the white men do when they want the lands of Indians.

(Black Hawk)

Then Curly's people 'removed from the plain with their families and lodges. They had heard the good news that the buffalo were numerous on the South Fork of the Platte.'

A Mormon's Cow
In the Moon of Making Fat, June of 1853, Curly's Hunkpatila band

Protected by the medicine items of his vision, Curly, at seventeen winters old, confronts two Arapaho warriors in the deed which earned him the name Crazy Horse, in Arapaho territory, Wyoming, summer 1858.

travelled with some Brulé to Laramie in order to collect their annuities. They were joined by some Miniconjou Lakota, who had not attended the Horse Creek Treaty, and felt even less bound by its rules than did the Oglala. On June 15th, a Miniconjou warrior loosed an arrow at a US sergeant as he crossed the Platte on the ferryboat. The commander at Fort Laramie, First Lieutenant Garnett, ordered the inexperienced brevet officer Lieutenant Fleming to arrest the warrior. Fleming promptly marched a detachment of infantry into the Lakota camp and shot dead three Miniconjou warriors. The Oglala and Brulé elders managed to pacify their guests, though the situation was not helped by Garnett's refusal to comply with the Lakota tradition of offering gifts as compensation for the killings.

The following summer of 1854, the Lakota once again gathered at Fort Laramie. Curly camped with some Brulé and with Man Afraid of His Horses, the Hunkpatila headman and leading chief of the Oglala, on the Platte six miles south of Fort Laramie. On 17th August, a small train of Mormon settlers passed the camp, one of them struggling behind, driving a worn out cow. The beast suddenly bolted into the Brulé camp circle where High Forehead, a Miniconjou warrior, shot an arrow through it. The frightened Mormon hurried away to demand compensation at Fort Laramie. The Lakota, awaiting the agent to distribute their overdue annuities, butchered the cow.

Conquering Bear was summoned to Fort Laramie by Fleming, who though only twenty-eight, was in command of the post. Conquering Bear offered to pay for the cow with ponies from his own herd, but Fleming demanded that the cow killer be turned over to him. He was urged on by Lieutenant John L. Grattan, a twenty-four year old fresh from West Point, who had boasted drunkenly that with thirty men he could whip the entire Sioux nation.

Conquering Bear told Fleming that the Miniconjou was a guest in his village, and that if Fleming wanted to arrest him he must do it himself. Fleming then ordered the hot-headed Grattan to arrest High Forehead 'if practicable and without unnecessary risks'.

Grattan, greatly excited, raised thirty volunteers for dangerous service, and set out on 19th August 1854, armed with a 12-pound field piece and a mountain howitzer, to 'conquer or die'.

The soldiers travelled east along the Oregon Trail to the trading post of James Bordeaux, three hundred yards from the Brulé camp. Here the Lakota chiefs Conquering Bear, Man Afraid of His Horses, Grand Partisan and Little Thunder urged him to turn back. Ignoring them, Grattan deployed his men in a line at the open end of Conquering Bear's camp circle. The white man's 'paper chief' tried to calm the situation, but Grattan aimed his howitzers at High Forehead's tipi, while the Miniconjou warrior sent word that he was ready to die.

Grattan's interpreter was Auguste Lucien who was married into the

Brought before his tribal headmen, the Big Bellies, in 1865, Crazy Horse receives the ceremonial shirt of big-horn skins, signifying his investiture as a Shirt Wearer of the Oglala.

Lakota but disliked by them. As Grattan lined up his guns, Lucien was meanwhile racing his horse to give it a second wind, as the Indians did before battle. He had drunk two bottles of whiskey, and was shouting wildly that the Lakota were all women; the soldiers would kill them all and he would cut out their hearts and eat them! He would give them new ears so that they understood his words! As Man Afraid of His Horses brought Bordeaux to replace the drunken interpreter, Grattan ordered his men to fire the howitzer.

A shot tore into the top of the lodges, and a Brulé warrior fell to the ground. Conquering Bear restrained his warriors, but Grattan's soldiers fired both cannons, and unleashed a volley from their Springfield rifles. Conquering Bear fell, mortally wounded, and the Horse Creek Treaty was torn in two.

Grattan fell under a hail of arrows. Spotted Tail's Brulé warriors rushed from the ravine behind the camp, Red Cloud's Oglala from the northern bluffs, and Grattan's men fell under blows from clubs and knives. Lucien's Lakota brother-in-law loosed an arrow into each of the fallen interpreter's ears, saying, 'Next time you will hear when we tell you not to live with the soldiers'. Grattan's body was later found, pierced by twenty-four arrows.

The excited Lakota warriors raided Bordeaux's trading post, and took their annuities from Gratiot's store, where they were awaiting the agent's arrival. Overnight, the old chiefs calmed the warriors, and in the morning the Lakota camps hurried north, casting a great cloud of dust into the sky.

Curly rode with his mother's people, the Brulé, towards the Snake River. As they stopped to make camp, Curly, who had seen Conquering Bear cut down by the soldier bullets, now caught a glimpse of the dying chief, his eyes hollow, his skin jaundiced. Shocked and confused, Curly leapt on his pony and rode away, alone.

Crying For a Vision

The Lakota believed that a sacred force pervaded every aspect of their life, so that their very existence was sacred. Anything mysterious was called *wakan*; the omnipotent deity was the Great Spirit, Wakan Tanka. One of the sacred seven rites of the Oglala was Hanblechyapi – Crying For a Vision – through which a young man sought guidance from the Sacred Powers. After purifying himself and under guidance from a holy man, the visionary fasted until he received some portent of his sacred power or 'medicine'.

Curly, though, went out alone and unprepared. He hobbled his horse in a holy place, in the Nebraska sandhills, where the Oglala Roan Eagle had a pit for catching eagles. For three days, Curly lay on the gravel, stripped to his breech-cloth, staring into the sky, sharp stones between his toes to keep him awake. Finally, feeling unworthy of a vision, he

Lakota pipe of about 1885. The bowl is of catlinite, the wooden stem wrapped with quillwork and adorned with the bighorn, deer, turtle and buffalo – all important figures in the religion of the Plains tribes.

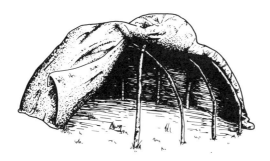

returned shakily to his horse. Suddenly, the earth reeled; with his stomach churning, Curly fell into the shade of a cottonwood tree.

He saw his horse start towards him, a light-haired man on its back. The horse was changing its hue, and floating above the ground. The man on its back wore a simple shirt and blue leggings. He had no face paint, and the central feather from a hawk's tail hung from his loose hair. A few beads adorned his scalp lock, and a small brown stone was tied behind one ear. He spoke no words, but Curly heard the warrior instruct him not to wear a war-bonnet or tie up his horse's tail before battle; Curly should also cast dust over his horse before fighting, and should never take anything for himself.

The man rode through a crowd of warriors, their arrows disappearing before they could hit him. Then he plunged into a fierce storm, now wearing only breechcloth and moccasins. Hailspots were dotted across his body, and a flash of lightning painted across his face. Over the man's head flew a red-backed hawk. The warrior's own people seemed to be holding him back, until they clasped his arms and engulfed him.

Then Curly awoke, being roughly shaken by his father, admonishing him for leaving camp alone.

It was three years before Curly told his father of his vision. Then the holy man, immersed in the scorching vapours of a sweat lodge, explained to his son that the vision he had seen was of himself, Curly. His father went on to say how he must dress as he had in the vision, a small stone behind his ear, a hawk over him. He must always be first in battle and through the power of thunder and the guidance of the hawk, he would be impervious to the bullets of his enemies. His path would be dark, but he should trust his vision, for it held great power.

Curly now had the Sacred Powers within him and continued to pray to them. Black Elk, the Oglala holy man, and Curly's cousin, described the powers graphically:

You have all heard of our great chief and priest Crazy Horse, but perhaps you did not know that he received most of his great power through the 'lamenting' which he did many times a year, and even in the winter, when it is very cold and very difficult. He received visions of the Rock, the Shadow, the Badger, a prancing horse, the Day, and also of Wanbli Galeshka, the Spotted Eagle, and from each of these he received much power and holiness.

In the sweat-lodge, a low dome of skins over a framework of willow saplings, the Indians purified themselves prior to religious rituals, in scorching vapours released by pouring water over red-hot rocks set in a central pit.

Crazy Horse – 'A Great Name'

The day after Curly's return to camp, Conquering Bear's body was wrapped in a buffalo robe and raised on a scaffold. In the Moon of Hairless Calves, 13th November, Conquering Bear's relatives Spotted Tail, Red Leaf and Long Chin avenged him by attacking a mail coach on the Holy Road, killing three white men.

Ignoring evidence to the contrary, Secretary of War Jefferson Davis declared the 'Grattan Massacre' to be the 'result of a deliberately formed plan' by the Lakota. A new agent from West Point, Thomas S. Twiss was appointed; and on 24th August 1855, General William S. Harney led a punitive expedition of six hundred men from Fort Kearney, Nebraska. The white-bearded general, later known as 'the Butcher', declared: 'By God, I'm for battle – no peace!'

Agent Twiss ordered all Lakota to move south of the Platte or be considered hostile. Most complied, but Little Thunder's Southern Brulé camp, which contained the lodges of Spotted Tail, Red Leaf and Curly's family, insisted on waiting for the meat from a buffalo hunt to dry.

On 3rd September, Harney marched his infantry into the camp on the Bluewater. Little Thunder parleyed while the women struck the lodges and prepared to flee; Harney talked while his cavalry secretly encircled the village. When the cavalry were discovered, the camp was thrown into confusion, and Harney's troops attacked the village without mercy.

Curly, away taming a mustang, returned to the camp only to witness the carnage left by the Butcher. Eighty-six of his people lay dead, including many children, and women with their dresses thrown back over their heads. The sight of so many relatives dead in their strong camp – unheard of among the Lakota who mourned even a single warrior's death – filled Curly with a bitterness that choked him.

Harney marched seventy women captives to Fort Laramie. There he withheld the Lakota annuities until 18th October, when Spotted Tail and the other mail-coach attackers, singing their death-songs, surrendered. They were imprisoned, and on the same day the humbled Lakota headmen touched the pen to another treaty at Fort Pierre.

Before the attack on the Blue Water, Curly had made his first kill at the age of thirteen. Joining a Brulé raid against the Omaha Indians, he saw an enemy sneaking through the undergrowth, and fired an arrow with great accuracy. Rushing to scalp his victim, Curly found it to be a woman. Although killing a woman was not considered disgraceful among the Lakota, Curly was sickened and left the scalp intact. On the journey home from this battle, in which the famous Omaha chief Logan Fontanelle was killed, the Lakota warriors teased Curly in song:

> A brave young man comes here,
> But a foolish one,
> Without a good knife

Magnificent Oglala eagle feather trailer bonnet. Only the tribe's ablest defenders claimed the right to wear such a bonnet. Imbued with the eagle's spiritual power, the bonnet was skilfully designed to sway and shimmer in the gentlest breeze, evoking the eagle's own movements.

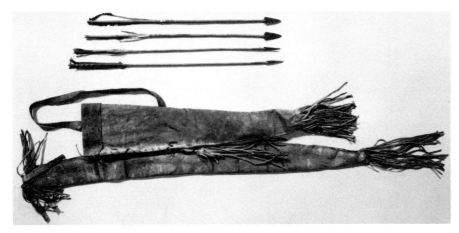

Curly was living with Cheyenne relatives in June 1857, when they were attacked on Solomon River by six troops of cavalry and three companies of infantry under Colonel Sumner. The Cheyenne medicine man Ice had given the warriors a sacred protection against the soldiers' bullets, but, ironically and inexplicably, Sumner ordered a sabre charge. The Cheyennes scattered in confusion, and Curly watched as yet another Indian village was put to the torch.

With a growing resentment towards the whites, Curly returned to his Oglala people. In the summer of 1857, they met with the Hunkpapa, Miniconjou, Sans Arcs, Blackfeet and Two Kettles tribes for a council at Bear Butte in the Black Hills. Only Spotted Tail's Brulé chose to stay away. As many as 7,500 Lakota gathered to declare their determination to unite against the white man's threat to their lands. When the earth grew bare, each band moved off for winter with a new gladness in its heart. Now Curly spoke to his father of his vision, and his adult life began.

Bowcase, quiver and arrows, probably Lakota. The bowcase and quiver are made from heavy, tanned skin, stained ochre brown and painted with green and red transverse lines. Such traditional weaponry of the warrior co-existed for some time with the repeater rifles.

A Warrior's Title
The Holy Road scared the buffalo away from the Black Hills. Consequently, the Oglala began to move north-west into the Powder River country. Though Old Smoke's Loafers remained at Fort Laramie, Red Cloud's Bad Faces, Red Dog's Oyukhpe, Sitting Bear's True Oglala and the Hunkpatila of Old Man Afraid of His Horses all migrated into the lands of their Miniconjou and Sans Arcs cousins. Horse Creek was forgotten as the Lakota warriors once more drove the Crow, Arapaho and Shoshoni from their lands.

In 1857, the Upper Platte Agency was moved from east of Laramie at Rawhide Butte Creek to Deer Creek on the North Platte, one hundred miles west of the fort. This agency suited the Powder River Lakota far more than those Indians still living near Laramie, though many whispered that Agent Twiss sold most of the Lakota annuity goods for his own gain.

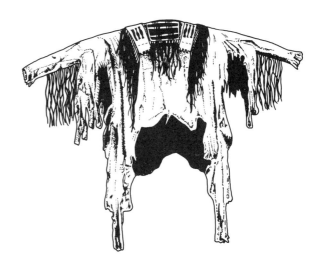

Lakota war-shirt (front and rear views) of antelope skin with legs and dew claws still attached, beaded at throat, quilled at shoulders and sleeves, and with pendants of human hair. Such hair fringes might symbolise the coups struck or scalps taken by a warrior, or the people of his own tribe that depended upon him. The shirt was, therefore, a symbol of bravery and rank.

In the summer of 1858, Curly, with his friends High Back Bone and Lone Bear, and his brother Little Hawk, joined a war-party against the Arapaho. They rode further west than Curly had ever been, into central Wyoming, where the Oglala 'wolves' or scouts discovered an Arapaho camp. Then, the warriors stripped to their breechcloths and prepared for war, dressing in preparation for death, and donning the medicine talismans that linked them with the Sacred Powers.

Curly tied a small, brown stone into his hair behind his ear, and hung an eagle bone whistle around his neck. He fastened a single hawk feather into his scalp-lock, so that his vision-spirit would be flying above him. This war medicine had been prepared by Curly's friend Chips, a holy man whose power came from visions of sacred stones. Scattering a handful of gopher dust over himself and his horse, Curly was prepared for war.

The Lakota were discovered heading toward the camp, and a few Arapaho warriors dug in behind some hill-top rocks, from where they held the Lakota at bay for nearly two hours. Suddenly, Curly urged his horse forward, and charged in amongst the Arapaho, counting coup. He charged them twice more, their arrows always missing – for he was now the man of his vision fighting in the *real world*, the sacred world. Two Arapaho rode out to meet him but Curly killed them both with arrows, then leaped down to take their scalps. This broke Curly's taboo never to take anything for himself, and with his medicine violated he felt an arrow crash into his leg. Curly limped to safety, and the war-party rode home.

At the victory dance that night, while the other Lakota warriors boasted of their deeds, Curly shied away.

'It was just his nature,' his friend He Dog recalled. 'He was a very quiet man, except when there was fighting'.

Curly's bravery, though, brought him great honour, Chips explained: 'When we were young all we thought about was going to war with some other nation; all tried to get their names up the highest, and whoever did

22

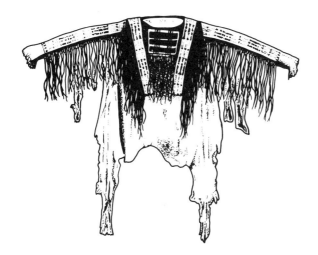

so was the principal man in the nation; and Crazy Horse wanted to get to the highest station and rank.'

Curly's father feasted the Hunkpatila headmen, announcing that he would now be known as Worm; then walked slowly among the lodges, singing:

> *My son has been against the people of unknown tongue,*
> *He has done a brave thing;*
> *For this I give him a new name, the name of his father,*
> *And of many fathers before him*
> *I give him a great name,*
> *I call him Crazy Horse.*

Respect, Vision and Anger

The following years were good ones for the Lakota living on the river they called the Powder, after the seams of lignite on its banks. The buffalo were plentiful, though another ocean of white emigrants swept across their lands in 1858, when gold was discovered in Colorado.

In 1860, John Loree, the new agent on the Upper Platte, relocated the Lakota agency back east of Laramie. The Loafers and the Corn band of the Brulé agreed to settle on a reservation; but the Powder River Lakota were furious when their annuity goods of 1863 became 'hoes and plows' instead of guns and bullets.

From 1861 to 1865, the white men fought amongst themselves, and their soldiers moved south. Following the 1862 Minnesota massacre of 450 whites by Santee warriors, volunteer troops were rushed to Fort Laramie. The time was ripe to drive the settlers from their lands, but the Lakota on the Powder seemed to have escaped the white man's evils, and were content to see the lodges fat with buffalo meat.

Crazy Horse grew to be a respected man during this time on the Powder. He carried much meat to his mother's lodge and was the bravest of the warriors in the raids against the Crow and Shoshoni. In the Moon of Making Fat, June 1861, he joined a party of Cheyenne and Lakota warriors in raiding the horse herd from Chief Washakie's Shoshoni on the Sweetwater River, Wyoming.

Crazy Horse and his younger brother were guarding the rear of their war party. After a lot of fighting, Crazy Horse's pony gave out. Crazy Horse turned it loose and the younger brother, who did not want to leave him, turned his own pony loose. Two of the enemy, mounted, appeared before them for single combat. Crazy Horse said to his brother, 'Take care of yourself – I'll do the fancy stunt.' Crazy Horse got the best of the first Shoshoni, the other one ran away. He got the horses of the two Shoshones and they caught up with the party. They had saved themselves and their party and got the two horses and the scalp of the Shoshone who was killed.

(Short Bull)

With such deeds, Crazy Horse became a popular leader of war-parties, all wishing to share his success and his strong medicine. He had acquired a new medicine, recalled by the brother of his first wife:

During war expeditions, he wore a little white stone with a hole through it on a buckskin string slung over his shoulder. He wore it under his left arm. He was wounded twice when he first began to fight but never since – after he got the stone. A man named Chips, a great friend of his, gave it to him.

(Red Feather)

Lakota medicine pouch of raw hide decorated with beadwork, holding a pebble. Stone-dreamer medicine was an important protective power, which Crazy Horse employed in battle.

Crazy Horse continued to lament and received a vision of the Thunder-beings, 'who come fearfully but bring goodness' as Black Elk described them. When flurrying snow filled the sky, Crazy Horse left camp alone to make the ancient snow-thunder medicine, finding that the snow-flakes, like the arrows of his enemies, could not touch him. Crazy Horse joined a medicine society called the Thunder Cult, and consequently rode into battle wearing only breechcloth and moccasins, his hair flying loose. He painted white hailspots across his chest and a forked zig-zag of lightning across his face to invoke his medicine. So prepared, he could not be harmed in battle, providing he always fought from the front, as He Dog recalled: 'Crazy Horse always led his men himself when they went into battle, and he kept well in front of them.'

In the summer of 1862, Crazy Horse stayed in the Bad Face Oglala camp, where he often stood with Black Buffalo Woman, niece of Red Cloud, their heads enfolded by a courting blanket. When Red Cloud sent word that he was to lead a war-party against the Crow, Crazy Horse joined up along with Little Hawk, High Back Bone, Lone Bear and the Bad Face brothers, No Water and Holy Bald Eagle (or Black Twin). As the warriors departed, No Water turned back, claiming that he had a toothache, bad medicine for a warrior whose power was derived from the teeth of the grizzly bear.

When the war-party returned two weeks later, singing victory songs, Crazy Horse learnt that No Water had married Black Buffalo Woman. His brother, Black Twin, was an influential man, and many people whispered that Red Cloud had arranged the marriage in order to bring power to his family. Crazy Horse rode away alone, returning with two

24

Crow scalps, which he threw to the dogs, for they were taboo to him. His anger and jealousy were to drive another wedge into the Oglala some years later.

Lighting the Flame

South of the Powder River, there were frequent clashes between the Cheyenne and volunteer soldiers who had replaced Civil War troops. Cheyenne headmen struggled to restrain their hot-blooded warriors, and Crazy Horse joined their attacks against emigrants still flooding along the Holy Road. Tension culminated on 29th November 1864 in a barbaric attack on friendly Cheyenne under Black Kettle, camped under a truce flag at Sand Creek. Colonel J.M. Chivington's 700 soldiers – including the Colorado Third's murderous 100-day volunteers – killed over 130 Cheyenne, mostly women and children. They mutilated the Indians' bodies, later displaying the Cheyenne women's pubic hair during the intermission of a Denver theatre show; the Plains were set aflame.

In December the Cheyenne sent the war-pipe to the Arapaho, Little Thunder's Southern Brulé and Bad Wound's Southern Oglala, who all smoked to indicate their participation in the war with the white man. Some nine hundred lodges from the various tribes gathered on Cherry Creek. Then they began moving slowly up the Platte, towards the Powder River Lakota. On 7th January 1865, a war-party of 1,000 warriors attacked Julesburg stage station, killing eighteen people. Crazy Horse joined a second attack on 2nd February, to plunder the station's remaining goods. In May, the Cheyenne joined the Oglala on Tongue River, while troops released from the Civil War reinforced the Platte.

The Oglala chiefs Two Face and Blackfoot now sought peace by taking a prisoner of the Cheyenne, Mrs Eubanks, to Fort Laramie. But their plan backfired; following her hysterical account of captivity, Laramie's temporary commander hanged the two chiefs. Their bodies, with artillery chains around their necks and iron balls dangling from their ankles, were left to swing from the fort's walls, driving the Lakota to fresh fury. Even the Loafers now fled to the Oglala camps, when the army attempted to march them unarmed to Fort Kearney in the heart of Pawnee territory.

That summer, the Lakota and Cheyenne performed their religious ceremonies together. Crazy Horse, who had eight horses shot from under him during his life, received from Chips a new protective stone to tie into his horse's tail. On 25th July 1865, he was one of twenty decoys who led an attack against the Platte Bridge stage station. Wearing his thunder medicine paint, Crazy Horse lured the station's troopers across the Platte towards 1000 concealed warriors. Impatiently, they sprung the trap prematurely, and the soldiers retreated safely. The following day, Crazy Horse led an attack against a relief column from the station, in which 29 troopers of the 11th Ohio Cavalry were killed.

Whilst not in Crazy Horse's nature to wear the flamboyant war bonnet, this unusual horn headdress has been attributed to him. It is a medicine bonnet of buffalo horns and hair, ermine, gold eagle wing pointers and 'fluffies', with owl and hawk feathers. It was used in ceremonies, dance, or perhaps in war to invoke its owner's guardian spirits.

25

The New Chief

That summer the southern half of the Northern Oglala renewed their chiefs. The people gathered around a great council lodge painted with sacred designs, in which sat the seven Wicasa Itacans, the greatest of the elders – the Big Bellies – with Old Man Afraid of His Horses seated in the middle. Then the chiefs of the warrior societies, finely dressed, rode through the village calling the names of those men selected to become the Wicasas or 'shirt-wearers'. The first three – American Horse, Young Man Afraid of His Horses and Sword – were all sons of Big Bellies. Then the warriors cried the name of a poor holy man's son, and the women trilled joyfully as Crazy Horse silently walked forward.

The people feasted and smoked before the four shirt-wearers each fastened a feather in their hair and donned their ceremonial shirts. These were made from two bighorn skins coloured with pigment in two halves, blue and yellow, or red and green. From Crazy Horse's quilled sleeves hung 240 hair-locks, symbolising his coups, and the people he was to protect. An old man instructed the shirt-wearers on their duties; to promote harmony, be generous, and always place the People before themselves. He Dog, who joined Red Cloud, Holy Bald Eagle and Big Road in the Bad Face's own investiture, recalled:

When we were made chiefs, we were bound by very strict rules as to what we should do and not do, which were very hard for us to follow. I have never spoken to any but a very few persons of what they made us promise then.

Red Cloud's War

Our nation is melting away like the snow on the sides of the hills where the Sun is warm, while your people are like the blades of grass in spring when the Summer is coming.
(Red Cloud, 1870)

In August 1865, three soldier columns under General Connor and Colonels Cole and Walker had invaded the Powder River country, under orders to kill 'every male Indian over twelve years of age'. While Connor established what would later become Fort Reno, Cole and Walker suffered repeated attacks from the Lakota including Crazy Horse. Their troops reached the fort in a state resembling that of a band of starving tramps rather than US soldiers. Governor Newton Edwards of Dakota Territory had meantime obtained treaty signatures from the already peaceful Lakota camps on the Missouri;

Like the old woman trying to catch the dog with a piece of meat in one hand and the butcher knife in the other.

(Sandoz)

'Winter of the Hundred Slain'

As part of President Grant's post-Civil War Peace Policy, the new treaty was sent to Colonel Maynardier at Fort Laramie. He was to obtain the hostile chiefs' signatures, guaranteeing the safety of miners following the Bozeman Trail to Montana. The council opened on June 13th 1866, with Red Cloud, Old Man Afraid and Spotted Tail all present. The Indians then learned of Colonel Henry B. Carrington's presence nearby. Carrington, with 700 men of the 18th Infantry, had marched from Fort Kearney, Nebraska with orders to establish forts on the Bozeman Trail regardless of the council's outcome.

Red Cloud stalked up to the commissioners, roaring: 'Great Father sends us presents and wants new road. But White Chief goes with soldiers to steal road before Indian says yes or no!'

The Oglala marched away, to defend their lands, while the friendly chiefs signed another meaningless treaty.

Carrington marched to Fort Reno, then on to the eastern foothills of the Bighorns. There, he began building Fort Phil Kearny, between Big Piney and Little Piney Creeks. In August he sent 150 men north to establish the third fort on the Bozeman Trail, Fort C.F. Smith on the Bighorn River. Red Cloud gathered 3000 warriors on the Tongue River, and between August and December of 1866, Lakota attacks claimed 154 lives and captured nearly 700 livestock. The Bozeman Trail was no safer than before, and wood or hay-cutting expeditions from Phil Kearny became treacherous undertakings.

In December, the Moon of Frost in the Tipi, the Miniconjou Chief White Swan died, after telling his people: 'Try to kill white men, for the white men have come here to kill you. I am about to die. I can kill no more. Therefore I look to you. Carry on.'

So the Miniconjou sent the war-pipe to the Oglala, who sent their finest warriors under Pawnee Killer and Crazy Horse to join a great attack on the fort. In attacks on the 6th and 19th December, the warriors had already discovered that the wood train was vulnerable to assaults from Lodge Trail Ridge north of the fort, beyond which nothing could be seen by the soldiers.

On the 20th December, some 2000 Oglala, Miniconjou, Brulé, Cheyenne and Arapaho warriors rode south along the Tongue. They wore blanket leggings and buffalo robes, with red Hudson's Bay blankets wrapped about their waists against the cold. On a snow-covered plain, the Lakota warriors formed a long line. From among them rode a *winkte*, a man who dressed and spoke like a woman, and was believed to hold *wakan* powers. With a black blanket drawn about his head, and blowing an eagle-bone whistle, the *winkte* rode his sorrel horse in zig-zags over a hill, searching for an enemy. He reappeared shortly, asking the Lakota chiefs, 'I have ten men, five in each hand; do you want them?' The chiefs said this was not enough. The *winkte* rode away and returned twice more, but the chiefs declined his offers of twenty and fifty men. When the *winkte* returned a fourth time, he fell from his horse, his

Lakota-type bow, quiver and bow case. The quiver and case are of deerskin, decorated with wool and beadwork. The bow is of recurved wood, further strengthened with sinew backing, with a string of sinew. Such short bows could loose arrows with great power and frequency from horseback, and were often preferred to firearms before the introduction of repeating rifles.

hands falling heavily to the ground. He shrieked, 'Answer me quickly, I have a hundred or more,' and the warriors, with a roar, began to count coup over the *winkte* in anticipation of the hundred victims he had delivered.

On the morning of 21st December 1866, the warriors prepared for war, Crazy Horse painting the lightning across his face but keeping his blanket tied around him against the cold. At the fork of Prairie Dog Creek, the Lakota chiefs Black Shield and Black Leg selected two warriors from each tribe to act as decoys – and Crazy Horse received the great honour of leading them.

The main war-party rode south-west, crossed the Bozeman Trail, and concealed themselves behind Lodge Trail Ridge. A smaller group circled westwards along the valley between the ridge and the Bighorns, to await the wood train travelling west below the Sullivant Hills. The wood train left late in the morning and, when attacked, corralled some 1½ miles from Fort Phil Kearny. Carrington prepared a relief force under the command of William J. Fetterman, who had once boasted, 'Give me eighty men and I would ride through the whole Sioux nation.' Carrington ordered him to: 'Support the wood train, relieve it, and report to me. Do not engage or pursue Indians at its expense. Under no circumstances pursue over the ridge . . .'

Fetterman led exactly 80 men from the fort. As they emerged, the Indians attacking the wood train withdrew, and Crazy Horse led the decoys over Lodge Trail Ridge. They were scattered by a shot from the fort's howitzer, but Crazy Horse feinted towards Fetterman, waving his red blanket. He slapped his horse with one hand, restraining it with the other, and Fetterman pursued him eagerly.

Retreating slowly, the decoys led the soldiers over the ridge, beyond sight of the fort, and up to Reno Creek. As the cavalry broke away to give chase, the decoys rode in zig-zags to signal the attack. The uncharacteristically well-disciplined Indians now broke from cover, 2000 warriors sweeping up behind the soldiers.

Two Lakota were killed as they charged in to count coup on the infantry. Then the sky was darkened with arrows, and the walking soldiers all fell. Fetterman raised his revolver to his temple and squeezed the trigger.

Some 400 yards to the north, the cavalry fought to the top of the ridge, and released their horses. The Indians clambered slowly up the slippery slope before mounting a charge. Then the last of the soldiers were clubbed to the ground, their blood freezing as it met the icy air.

The warriors stripped the soldiers and mutilated their bodies terribly. A dog seen running from the scene was impaled with an arrow, in order that nothing at all of the enemy force should survive. Crazy Horse, who had been prominent in the fighting, now held Lone Bear in his arms, as his friend died from his wounds. He mourned for the dead Lakota, but it

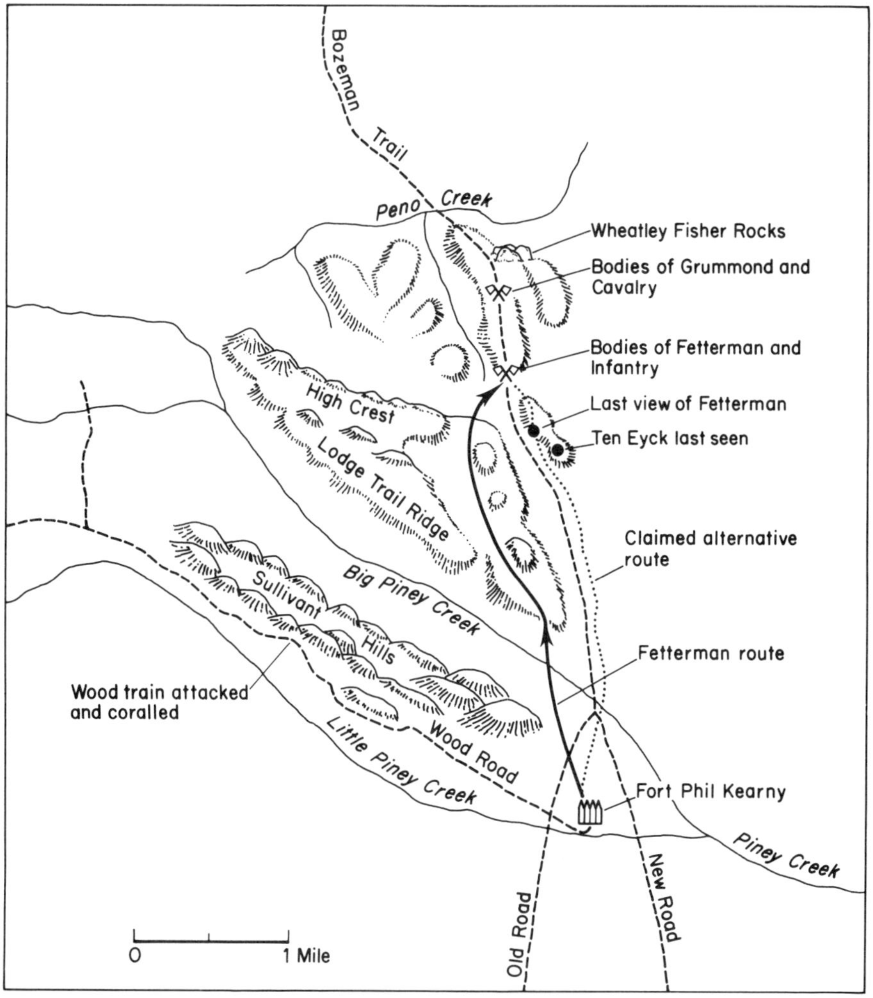
Bozeman Trail
Peno Creek
Wheatley Fisher Rocks
Bodies of Grummond and Cavalry
Bodies of Fetterman and Infantry
Last view of Fetterman
Ten Eyck last seen
High Crest
Lodge Trail Ridge
Claimed alternative route
Big Piney Creek
Sullivant Hills
Fetterman route
Wood train attacked and coralled
Wood Road
Little Piney Creek
Fort Phil Kearny
Piney Creek
Old Road
New Road
0
1 Mile

had been a good day to die. The whites would call the battle 'the Fetterman Massacre'; but Crazy Horse, because of the *winkte* prophecy, called it 'the Battle of the Hundred Slain'.

The Battle of the Hundred Slain – the Fetterman Massacre – Fort Phil Kearny, 21 December, 1866.

The Wagon Box Fight

Instead of attacking Fort Phil Kearny, the Indians now divided, seeking shelter from the winter snows. The U.S. government reacted with horror to the worst defeat to date of the Army in the Indian Wars; and Carrington was relieved of his command on 23rd January 1867. While the friendly Lakota signed another treaty in April, Crazy Horse led raids near Fort Reno. In the summer, the hostiles gathered for their Sun Dance, and took the war 'out of the bag' once more. In July, the Cheyenne went north to attack Fort C.F. Smith, while Crazy Horse and Young Man Afraid led 500 Lakota against Fort Phil Kearny.

Crazy Horse again led the decoys in attacking a wood-cutting party. His purpose was to draw the soldiers from a corral of wagon boxes that had been constructed west of the fort. However, the main body of warriors raced from hiding prematurely, intent upon capture of the fort's horse herd. The woodcutters escaped to the fort under covering fire from the wagon boxes. The Lakota circled the corral, but were held at bay by Captain James Powell and 30 men armed with the new Springfield breech-loading rifles and delivering a withering cross fire.

The warriors withdrew, and Crazy Horse formed them into a slowly advancing wedge on foot. One soldier later said, 'It chilled my blood . . . hundreds and hundreds of Indians swarming up a ravine about ninety yards to the west of the corral . . . it looked for a minute as though our last moment on earth had come.' Yet the Lakota could not reach the corral, and when reinforcements appeared from the fort, Crazy Horse had to withdraw. This, the Wagon Box Fight of 2nd August 1867, was almost a repetition of the Hayfield Fight of the previous day, with the Cheyenne turned back by the superior fire-power at Fort C.F. Smith.

The government, though, had grown tired of the expenditure of lives and money on Red Cloud's War. A new peace commission met with Old Man Afraid in November, then returned with a wagon-load of goods for Red Cloud in April 1868. While the government representatives kicked their heels, Red Cloud sent a message, saying: 'We are on the mountains looking down on the soldiers and the forts. When we see the soldiers moving away and the forts abandoned, then I will come down and talk.' On 27th July, Fort C.F. Smith was abandoned, and was set ablaze by Crazy Horse's warriors the following dawn. Some days later, Little Wolf's Cheyenne burned Fort Phil Kearny to the ground. Red Cloud finally arrived at Laramie on 4th November. He 'washed his hands with the dust of the floor' and touched the pen to the 1868 Laramie Treaty. This established a Lakota reservation spanning South Dakota and declared the Powder River country 'unceded Indian territory'. It also instructed the Indians to settle on farms; this Red Cloud ignored, departing to hunt on the Powder once more.

Crazy Horse never came to Fort Laramie, instead leading his camp north-east to join Sitting Bull's Hunkpapa. Here He Dog recounted, 'the older more responsible men of the tribe conferred another kind of chieftainship on Crazy Horse. He was made war chief of the whole Oglala tribe. A similar office was conferred on Sitting Bull by the Hunkpapa tribe.'

Defending the Black Hills

Crazy Horse led raids against the Crow in the summer of 1869. He quickly comprehended the Laramie treaty's implications when he attempted to trade for powder and lead on the Platte and was fired on by soldiers. The Indians had either to move on to a reservation, or stay on Powder River without trading; and Crazy Horse naturally took the second option.

The following summer, Crazy Horse and He Dog led a raid against the Crow, east of the Big Horns:

> When we came back, the people came out of the camp to meet us and escorted us back, and at a big ceremony presented us with two spears, the gift of the whole tribe, which was met together. These spears were each three or four hundred years old and were given by the older generation to those in the younger generation who had best lived the life of a warrior.
>
> (He Dog)

In the next raid against the Crow, Crazy Horse and He Dog were elected lance-bearers of the Kangi Yuha or Crow-Owners, one of the Oglala warrior societies. Such officership was accorded great honour and carried special obligations in battle. When the raiders reached the Crow reservation, Crazy Horse took the crow-skin society lance from its case and passed it over the smoke of a sweetgrass fire. The lance's red-painted shaft was wrapped in otter fur, with eagle and owl feathers at one end; below its spear-head was bound the stuffed skin of a crow.

The Bad Heart Bull manuscript records Crazy Horse's first conflict as a lance-bearer as the battle 'When They Chased the Crows Back to Camp'. He Dog led the Lakota in stealing the Crow camp's horses, the Crow warriors making a determined pursuit. Crazy Horse, as a crow-lance bearer, was obliged never to retreat, and rallied his men. They countercharged, driving the enemy back amongst their own lodges, and lifting thirteen scalps. A Crow captive later said that his people 'knew Crazy Horse had a medicine-gun that never missed, and that he was bullet-proof.'

Black Buffalo Woman

Ten days after this battle, while No Water was away hunting, Crazy Horse rode from his Oglala camp with Black Buffalo Woman at his side. When No Water returned, he pursued and caught up with the eloping couple on the Powder. Borrowing a revolver from Bad Heart Bull, No Water burst into the lodge, where the two were seated with friends including Little Big Man and He Dog's brother, Little Shield.

'My friend, I have come!' cried No Water and shot Crazy Horse in the face from only four feet away. His upper jaw shattered, Crazy Horse slumped forward into the fire.

No Water fled, telling his friends that he had killed the Hunkpatila

Rear view of a magnificent southern Lakota war-shirt of about 1870. Originally accredited to Crazy Horse, the Nebraska State Historical Society now associate the shirt with Greasing Hand, because it was acquired at Pine Ridge Agency, which was established in 1878 after Crazy Horse's murder. Greasing Hand married Crazy Horse's widow Nellie Larrabee, and, settling at Pine Ridge, assumed his predecessor's name; though it is not inconceivable that he also inherited Crazy Horse's shirt. Whatever its history, the shirt is a good example of the type presented to Crazy Horse upon his election as a Shirt Wearer. It has a blue-dyed upper, and yellow-dyed lower half, and is adorned with 291 hair-locks. The predominantly white beadwork, with red crosses, and dark green panels with red lines and borders of blue triangles is typical of the Southern Lakota.

shirt-wearer. They built him a sweat lodge in order to purify him of the murder. Meanwhile, Crazy Horse's followers, unable to find No Water, shot the mule he had left behind, and Crazy Horse himself was carried to the lodge of his uncle Spotted Crow.

The Oglala circle again lay shattered, and the Hunkpatila demanded that No Water be turned over to them. No Water sheltered in the Bad Face camp of Holy Bald Eagle, who told him, 'Come and stay with me and if they want to fight us, we will fight.'

An internecine struggle was prevented only by the mediation of Crazy Horse's uncles, who sent Black Buffalo Woman to Bad Heart Bull's lodge to be returned to No Water. She later gave birth to a light-haired girl, whispered to be Crazy Horse's daughter. But when No Water sent three ponies to Worm, the matter was supposedly closed.

Crazy Horse slowly recovered, a scar remaining below his left nostril. He later met No Water on a hunting trip, and pursued him all the way to the Yellowstone; after which No Water took to living at Red Cloud Agency. The repercussions of the incident were serious, for the Big Bellies decreed that Crazy Horse had put his interests before those of the tribe, and must return his ceremonial shirt.

Because of all this, Crazy Horse could not be a shirt-wearer any longer. When we were made chiefs we were bound by very strict rules . . . I have always kept the oaths I made then, but Crazy Horse did not . . . The shirt was never given to anybody else. Everything seemed to stop right there. Everything began to fall to pieces. After that it

In the 'Battle Where They Chased The Crows Back To Camp', of 1870, the Lakota are led by Crazy Horse, his status indicated by carrying the ancient Crow-lance of the Kangi Tuha or Crow-Owners warrior society.

seemed as if anybody who wanted to could wear the shirt – it meant nothing. But in the days when Crazy Horse and I received the shirts, we had to accomplish many things to win them.

(He Dog)

As he recovered, Crazy Horse took a new wife, Black Shawl, but soon suffered a new blackness in his heart. A war-party returned from south of the Platte to report the death of his brother Little Hawk, shot by white miners. Wearily, Crazy Horse rode south, found his brother's body, and raised it on a scaffold.

When the summer was passed, Crazy Horse and High Back Bone led a large party against the Shoshoni. Finding the ground at Wind River treacherous, Crazy Horse asked, 'I wonder if we can make it back to Cone Creek? I doubt if our horses can stand in this slush. They sink in over their ankles.'

Angrily, High Back Bone replied: 'This is the second fight he has called off in this same place! This time there is going to be a fight. The last time you called off a fight here, when we got back to camp they all laughed at us. You and I have our good name to think about. If you don't care about it you can go back. But I'm going to stay here and fight.'

Reluctantly, Crazy Horse acquiesced, but the two *kolas* were soon guarding a Lakota retreat. High Back Bone's horse was wounded and a Shoshoni charge engulfed the great warrior.

Seeking High Back Bone's body, Crazy Horse returned four days later, but found only bones left by the coyotes. After losing his chieftainship, his brother and his greatest friend, he would now fight with no fear of death.

Skirmish with Longhair

In the spring of 1871, Crazy Horse's Oglala band drifted northward, strengthening their relations on the Yellowstone with the northern Lakota, the Hunkpapa, Miniconjou and Sans Arcs. There, Black Shawl gave birth to Crazy Horse's daughter, who was called They Are Afraid of Her.

In the summer that followed, Crazy Horse fought in the Second Arrow Creek Fight, called the 'Time When Yellow Shirt Was Killed by the Crow'. Crazy Horse is depicted at this battle in the Bad Heart Bull manuscript, wearing breech-cloth, moccasins and a cape, and shown leaving his wounded horse. This is confirmed:

Crazy Horse charged the Crows, his horse was shot under him, and he was surrounded by the enemy. The Oglala tried to help him but could not get near him. A man named Spotted Deer made a last effort to reach him. He broke through the enemy and Crazy Horse got on to his pony behind him and they made a charge for the open. They made it back to the Sioux lines, riding double and closely pursued.

(Short Bull)

That August, a surveying party protected by Major E.M. Baker's 2nd

---

Seized by Little Big Man, as foretold in his vision, Crazy Horse receives a fatal thrust from the bayonet of Private William Gentles, outside Fort Robinson guard house, 5th September 1877.

Cavalry, plotted the Northern Pacific Railroad's continuation along the Yellowstone. They fought a long-range engagement with Sitting Bull and Crazy Horse on the fourteenth, and were eventually turned back.

In the winter, Crazy Horse's following fell to about fifty lodges, but increased to some 200 when the agency Indians came north for the buffalo and the Sun Dance the following summer.

A new surveying party hammered stakes along the Yellowstone in June 1873, protected by General D.S. Stanley's troops, and the 7th Cavalry of General Custer, who the Indians called Pahuska, or Long Hair. On 4th August, Crazy Horse and five other decoys attacked Custer's advance party of some ninety men. When Long Hair refused to be drawn, 300 Indian warriors burst from cover and drove the soldiers back into a grove near the mouth of Tongue River. When Custer eventually counter-attacked, his heavy cavalry horses were outrun by the Indians' fleet-footed ponies.

There were skirmishes for the next seven days, before the Indians forded the Yellowstone, a manoeuvre beyond the troopers' capabilities. At dawn on 11th August, the Lakota warriors re-crossed the river, killing four soldiers and shooting Long Hair's horse from beneath him, before being driven off. The surveyors returned east, where their work came to nothing with the bankruptcy of the Northern Pacific Railroad. Meanwhile, Crazy Horse wintered on the Powder.

The Thieves' Trail

In 1874, rumours began to circulate among the white settlements that there was gold in the Black Hills. Though the 1868 Laramie Treaty guaranteed this land to the Indians 'so long as the grass shall grow', General Sheridan sent an expedition to investigate. On 2nd July, Long Hair led 1200 men, including miners and geologists, from Fort Abraham Lincoln on the Missouri, into Pa Sapa. He sent back reports telling of gold 'from the grass roots down,' precipitating a gold rush into the Lakota lands. Custer also commented that he 'could whip all the Indians in the north-west with the Seventh Cavalry.' The Lakota now called Long Hair 'thief' and the route he had taken 'the Thieves' Road'.

Crazy Horse had a more personal cause for grief. When he returned from raiding the Crow, he found Black Shawl with her hair cut and her dress ripped in mourning – and his daughter dead from cholera. He rode to Crow country to find the scaffold that held her tiny body, and mourned for three days.

Unrest about the Black Hills invasion grew at Red Cloud Agency, and many Lakota rode out to join Crazy Horse at the summer's end, taking their allegiance away from Red Cloud forever. Buffalo were scarce that harsh winter, but in the spring Crazy Horse led the Lakota and Cheyenne in frequent attacks against the miners that were flocking into Pa Sapa's heart. In the summer of 1875, Crazy Horse's Oglala, Sitting Bull's

Hunkpapa, Spotted Eagle's Sans Arcs, and Miniconjou under Touch the Clouds, all joined the Cheyenne in a great Sun Dance.

At the end of summer, Young Man Afraid and the interpreter Louis Richards brought tobacco to Crazy Horse's camp, asking him to meet a commission from Washington at Red Cloud Agency. Crazy Horse said simply, 'One does not sell the earth upon which the people walk.'

The council opened on 20th September, eight miles east of the Lakota agency, with twenty thousand Lakota, Cheyenne and Arapaho present. Senator William Allison proposed the purchase of mining rights for the Black Hills, and gave the Indians three days in which to discuss the matter. They reconvened on 23rd September, each band's warriors galloping down from the hills firing their guns, until thousands of Indians surrounded the commissioners' council tent.

About noon, Red Cloud prepared to open the council. There was a sudden movement in the Indian ranks; Little Big Man, Crazy Horse's emissary, burst from among the warriors. Mounted on a fine, grey pony, wearing only breech-cloth and war-bonnet, blood ran down his chest from the freshly opened scars of the Sun Dance. Brandishing a Winchester and shells, and with two revolvers in his belt, Little Big Man declared that he was going to kill the white men who had come to steal the Lakota lands.

The Indian police immediately overpowered him, but only Young Man Afraid's dignified entreaties quieted the excited warriors.

The commissioners quickly scuttled back to Fort Robinson, and Crazy Horse's voice had been heard. On 20th September the commissioners proposed to purchase the hills for $6,000,000, but were told by Spotted Tail that the price was too small. The Lakota left the agencies in large numbers to join the Powder River camps as it became clear that the whites, unable to purchase the Black Hills, would try to steal them.

The commissioners recommended that 'if the Government will interpose its power and authority, they (the Indians) are not in a position to resist.' On 3rd November, President Grant told General Sheridan that the Indians must be forced on to the reservations so as to solve the Black Hills problem. On 9th November, Indian Inspector E.C. Watkins toured the Lakota lands and recommended that the government 'send troops against them in the winter . . . and whip them into subjection.'

Thus, on 6th December, Red Cloud Agent James Hastings was instructed to send messengers to the Lakota, notifying them that 'unless they shall remove within the lands of their reservation (and remain there) before the 31st January, they shall be deemed hostile, and treated accordingly by the military force.'

Indian runners battled through blizzards to Crazy Horse's camp on the Tongue, where Black Twin told them the snow was too deep and the ponies too thin for the camp to move into the reservation. Then Crazy Horse led his people north to join Sitting Bull.

Eagle talon medicine bundle adorned with cloth and beadwork wrapping with brass bells. This magnificent talisman conveyed the eagle's power to strike its prey to a warrior who had received such a blessing in a vision-quest. Such symbols of medicine remained important to a visionary like Crazy Horse for the whole of his life.

On 8th February 1876, Sheridan ordered Generals Crook and Terry to prepare for military operations on the Powder, Tongue, Rosebud and Bighorn headwaters 'where Crazy Horse and his allies frequented.'

As spring brought fresh herds of buffalo, He Dog took a dozen lodges to join Old Bear's Cheyenne camp – and on 17th March 1876, Crook's advance force of six cavalry companies under Colonel J.J. Reynolds fell upon the camp. The Indians fled, while the soldiers burned their lodges and possessions. Mistakenly, the troops believed they had destroyed the camp of Crazy Horse, whom Captain J.G. Bourke described as, 'justly regarded as the boldest, bravest and most skilful warrior in the whole Sioux nation.'

It was, though, Crazy Horse's village that took in the refugees after a flight of three days. The Oglala headmen cried out 'Cheyenne, come and eat here', while Crazy Horse told them, 'I'm glad you are come. We are going to fight the white man again.'

Short Bull later said, 'If it had not been for that attack by Crook on Powder River, we would have come in to the agency that spring, and there would have been no Sioux war.'

Greatest Victory

Crazy Horse led his people north to join the ever growing camp of Sitting Bull. This great camp lumbered on to new grass every few days; as they moved, another cluster of horses would haul their travois into the long column, bringing families fresh from the agencies. By May, the Rosebud valley was filled with lodges. In June, Sitting Bull offered one hundred pieces of flesh at the Hunkpapa Sun Dance and received a vision of many soldiers falling into camp. Wakan Tanka told him: 'I give you these because they have no ears.'

Rosebud
After the Sun Dance, the camp moved to Ash Creek on the Little Bighorn, where Cheyenne scouts rode in howling like wolves, proclaiming the discovery of many Blue Coats on the Rosebud. These were the 1,047 soldiers under Crook that had marched north from Fort Fetterman on 20th May, with 262 Crow and Shoshoni scouts. Meanwhile, 460 men under Colonel John Gibbon, were marching east along the Yellowstone from Fort Ellis, Montana; and 925 men including Custer's 7th Cavalry were marching west from Fort Abraham Lincoln under Brigadier-General Alfred Terry.

On 16th June, Crazy Horse led a force of at least 1,500 warriors against Crook. Nearing the headwaters of the Rosebud at dawn on 17th June 1876, he stopped to prepare for battle, applying his snow-thunder paint and fastening the stuffed skin of a red-backed hawk in his hair.

Crook's forces were camped on both sides of the Rosebud and the first intimation they received of danger was the appearance of an Indian scout, screaming, 'Lakota! Lakota!' Crazy Horse, the majority of his warriors concealed behind bluffs, led the first attack from the north-west, but was held by the Crow and Shoshoni scouts. Then the infantry's arrival pushed the Lakota back to a ridge a mile north of Rosebud Creek. The Indians then attacked further east, but were driven west by a cavalry charge under Captain Mills. They rallied on a second line of hills, making bravery runs, slapping their buttocks and taunting the soldiers. The correspondent John Finerty reported, 'One chief, probably the late, lamented Crazy Horse, directed their movements by signals made with a pocket mirror . . .'

The soldiers drove the Indians back from a second ridge, then a third, only to see their ranks arrayed on the next crest. Colonel Royall's men became surrounded on a south-easterly hill, while the Indian scouts, supported by cavalry, drove the Lakota westwards. Crook's remaining troops skirmished on the edge of the valley:

He Dog, a life-long friend of Crazy Horse, pictured in 1930 when, aged ninety-two, he provided Eleanor Hinman with a remarkable history of his comrade the Oglala chief. His memory of events gave him the status and rôle of tribal chronicler. Other old-timers, when interviewed, often simply replied: 'He Dog will remember that'.

The soldiers first got the Sioux and the Cheyenne on the run. Crazy Horse, Bad Heart Bull, Black Deer, Kicking Bear and Good Weasel rallied the Sioux, turned the charge, and got the soldiers on the run. When these five commenced to rally their men that was as far as the soldiers got.

(Short Bull)

In one clash, Jack Red Cloud, son of Oglala chief Red Cloud, was surrounded by Crow scouts, who snatched off his war-bonnet, which he had no right to wear, and whipped him. They laughed at his pleas for mercy, until Crazy Horse swept down and snatched the boy to safety.

Crook drew his men into a tighter circle, while his snipers pinned down the Indians from a ridge in the north-west, and the 9th Infantry supported Royall. Then he ordered Mills to go north, along a thin defile towards where he believed the Indian camp to be. Crazy Horse – crying 'today is a good day to fight, today is a good day to die,' – led a fresh onslaught against Crook's weakened force. Only by recalling Mills, who swept around into the Indians' flank, did Crook save his command.

The warriors withdrew, having demonstrated a new determination and co-ordination in their fighting. Crook claimed a victory, but had lost 28 dead with 56 wounded – and expended 25,000 rounds of ammunition and all his supplies. He was out of the summer campaign, returning to his Goose Creek base camp, where he stayed until July, licking his wounds.

Battle On The Greasy Grass

Six nights after the Rosebud battle, the Indians found a new campsite, their smoke-tinted tipis stretching for three miles along the west bank of the Little Bighorn, in the valley they called the Greasy Grass. Ten thousand people gathered there. The Cheyenne camped in the north,

Carbine of 1873 and purported to be used by Crazy Horse to kill the last of Custer's troops.

then the Brulé, Sans Arcs, Oglala, Blackfoot and Miniconjou circles, with the Hunkpapa in the south.

Terry and Gibbon had met up above Rosebud Creek, aware of the Indian camp on the Little Bighorn, but oblivious to Crook's defeat. Councilling on the steamer *Far West*, they proposed to surround the camp by sending Custer south while Gibbon swept west and attacked from the north. On 22nd June, Custer led 31 officers and 586 soldiers of the 7th Cavalry, with 33 Indian scouts and 20 civilians, south along the Rosebud. He had turned down the offer of three cumbersome Gatling guns and four troops of the 2nd Cavalry, and carried rations for only fifteen days. As they departed, Gibbon remarked, 'Now Custer, don't be greedy but wait for us.' Custer replied, ambiguously, 'No, I will not.'

When his scouts found the Indian village's trail, Custer swung west immediately, making a forced march on the night of 24th June. His scouts became animated over their discovery of sandpictures, depicting Sitting Bull's vision; and the Arikara warrior Bloody Knife warned that the camp held more Indians than the soldiers had bullets. Nevertheless, at noon on Sunday 25th June 1876, Custer prepared to attack the village, hidden to the west behind bluffs and trees. Leaving the pack-train behind, he divided his men into three groups: Captain F.W. Benteen scouted south-west with 113 men; Major M.A. Reno took 131 men south; Custer hurried north with 215 men, along the bluffs above the valley in which the camp lay.

Lakota women, digging turnips, alerted the camp to Long Hair's presence, and the warriors dressed hurriedly for death. Suddenly at about 3.00 p.m., Reno's men hit the southern end of the village, cutting down those women and children standing out in the open. The Hunkpapa rallied and turned Reno's hesitant charge. Crazy Horse 'rode with the greatest daring' up and down in front of Reno's skirmish line and as soon as these troops were driven across the river, he went at once to Custer's front and 'there became the leading spirit.' Reno's men were driven across the Little Bighorn, digging in to the bluffs where they were supported by Benteen's arrival at 4.15 p.m.

Short Bull first saw Crazy Horse after Reno's retreat:

'Too late! You've missed the fight!' we called out to him. 'Sorry to miss the fight!' he laughed, 'but there's a good fight coming over the hill.'

I looked where he pointed and saw Custer and his blue coats pouring over the hill. I thought there were a million of them.

'That's where the big fight is going to be,' said Crazy Horse, 'We'll not miss that one.' He was not a bit excited; he made a joke of it. He wheeled and rode down the river, and a little while later I saw him on his pinto pony leading his men across the ford. He was the first man to cross the river. I saw he had the business well in hand. They rode up the draw and then there was too much dust – I could not see any more.

As Custer continued along the eastern bluffs, he was turned away by warriors led by the Hunkpapa Gall, and forced to continue north. Crazy Horse swept through the heart of the Indian camp, hearing a growing thunder of hooves behind him. He emerged from the Cheyenne camp with a thousand warriors at his heels, and galloped across the ford, encircling Long Hair.

Custer's troops were retiring 'step by step' from Gall's attack. Lieutenant Calhoun's L Company was engulfed, and the Companies of Lieutenant A.E. Smith and Captain Thomas Custer were swept into Deep Coulee Ravine. Meanwhile, Long Hair Custer, with Captain G.W. Yates' Company, was ascending the highest point on the ridge –

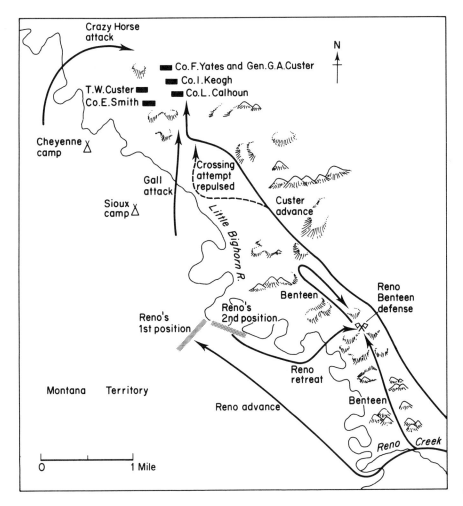

The Battle on the Greasy Grass – the Little Bighorn – fought on 25th June, 1876.

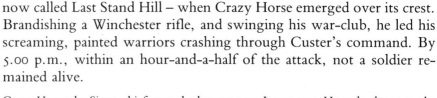

now called Last Stand Hill – when Crazy Horse emerged over its crest. Brandishing a Winchester rifle, and swinging his war-club, he led his screaming, painted warriors crashing through Custer's command. By 5.00 p.m., within an hour-and-a-half of the attack, not a soldier remained alive.

Crazy Horse the Sioux chief, was the bravest man I ever saw. He rode closest to the soldiers, yelling to his warriors. All the soldiers were shooting at him, but he was never hit.

(Arapaho Warrior)

Reno and Benteen remained entrenched through the night, and when the wolves reported Gibbon's approach the next day, the Indian camp moved off towards the Bighorns. Crazy Horse rode off alone to a butte near Reno Creek, and engraved in the sand a horse and a snake with lightning marks, the signs of his vision.

Lakota shield cover of tanned skin is painted with protective medicine designs, in black, white, yellow, red, green and bright blue; the central feature probably depicting the Eagle or Thunderbird. While a shield of rawhide padded with hair could deflect a low-velocity musketball, the importance of its medicine designs was such that sometimes only the flimsy, protective cover was carried into battle.

Surrender and Death

Inevitably, the huge Indian camp divided, and many Indians returned to the agencies. Here they were forced to sign away the Black Hills on threat of having their rations stopped. Crazy Horse renewed his attacks against the miners. Then, in August, Crook and Terry set out to hunt him once more. On 9th September 1876, Crook's advance detachment under Captain Mills struck a camp of Oglala and Miniconjou under Iron Plume. Most of the Lakota escaped, and Crazy Horse led a counterattack against Crook, but was fought off by superior numbers.

Crook returned from the field in October in order to enlist scouts from the Lakota agencies who would hunt for their own people in his winter campaign. Colonel Ranald Mackenzie was dispatched to find Crazy Horse; instead he struck Dull Knife's Cheyenne camp at dawn on 25th November. The Cheyenne suffered forty dead; losing all their belongings, they fled desperately through the snow. Twelve Cheyenne children froze in their mothers' arms on the first night of the flight, and eleven more nights passed before they reached the camp of Crazy Horse.

'We helped the Cheyennes the best we could. We hadn't much ourselves,' Short Bull recalled. Wooden Leg, the Cheyenne, remembered 'Oh, how generous were the Oglala!' Yet Bourke wrote that: 'Crazy Horse was indifferent to the sufferings of his allies, and turned the cold shoulder upon them completely.'

Certainly, from this time, the Cheyenne seemed to be the first of Crazy Horse's friends suddenly to turn against him.

The Oglala and Cheyenne village moved up the Tongue. With his people hungry, Crazy Horse sent a delegation under Packs The Drum (Sitting Bull) to seek terms with Colonel Miles at Fort Keogh. As they

Shield cover, bearing blue, red and yellow medicine symbols including the Thunderbird. It has been attributed to Crazy Horse and according to its documentation, it was captured by General Lawton, who 'might have been attached to Miles' Command.'

approached the fort under a white flag, Miles' Crow scouts shot down five of the Lakota, leaving them bleeding in the snow; so ending the peace talks.

Now, even Crazy Horse's own people tried to sneak away to the agencies, so that his faithful warriors had to shoot the horses of the renegades in order to make them stay.

Following skirmishes on 1st and 3rd January 1877, some 500 infantry under Miles struck Crazy Horse's camp on 8th January. Miles' faltering charge through deep snow was held by Crazy Horse and just three others, while the rest of the camp fled. A blizzard forced Miles back to Fort Keogh, Crazy Horse following him all the way in a forlorn attempt to rescue some captured women.

In January, Red Cloud's nephew Sword led an Oglala delegation from the agency to beg Crazy Horse's surrender; but he refused their tobacco. Then, the half-breed Big Leggins Johnny Brughier brought in the captured women with an offer that Crazy Horse should surrender to Miles.

In March, Spotted Tail led 250 Brulé to Crazy Horse's camp, with promises from Crook of the Oglala chief's own agency if Crazy Horse surrendered at Fort Robinson. Crazy Horse, seeing his people truly divided, stayed away from camp during Spotted Tail's visit. He left a message with Worm, saying he shook hands with his uncle, and would bring in his people when the weather permitted.

Spotted Tail, the outstanding Brulé headman, with his wife and daughter, in Nebraska about 1879. Though remembered as one of the most fearless of all Lakota warriors, Spotted Tail became a leading advocate for peace with the whites after 1864.

41

Crazy Horse councilled on the Powder River with Little Wolf, He Dog and Ice of the Cheyenne, and listened as old Iron Hawk told him: 'You see all the people here are in rags, they all need clothing, we may as well go in.' With the buffalo dying and his people's spirit broken, Crazy Horse headed towards the agency. Red Cloud met him on 27th April, saying, 'All is well; have no fear; come on in.' Thus he stole the 'honour' of Crazy Horse's capture from Spotted Tail.

On the morning of 6th May 1877, Crazy Horse met Lieutenant 'White Hat' Clark, commanding officer at Red Cloud Agency, some seven miles out from the agency. Crazy Horse smoked with Clark, then held out his left hand, saying: '*Kola*, I shake with this hand because my heart is on this side; I want this peace to last forever.' He then gave his war-shirt to Red Cloud.

Shortly after noon, Crazy Horse's people approached the agency, led by Clark and Red Cloud's Indian police. At Crazy Horse's side rode He Dog, Little Hawk, Little Big Man, Old Hawk and Bad Road; and behind them rode a finely disciplined column of warriors, painted and dressed in their finest costume. For two miles behind them, the women and children rode in silence, the hooves of 2,000 Oglala ponies rumbling across the ground. Nearing the fort, Crazy Horse began to sing, softly and deeply, the peace song of the Lakota. All the warriors took up the chant, then the women and children, until the voice of nearly 900 people echoed through the valley. 'By God! This is a triumphal march, not a surrender!' one officer remarked.

While the Oglala women raised the lodges on the banks of the White River, the warriors surrendered their ponies to Red Cloud's eager followers. Then Clark searched the Oglala lodges, confiscating 117 guns, including Crazy Horse's three Winchesters. Clark was all the while guarded by his Cheyenne scouts. Crazy Horse's old friends, including Little Wolf and Morning Star, were hidden, painted for war, behind a ridge; waiting to attack the Oglala.

Of his surrender, Luther Standing Bear said that Crazy Horse, 'foresaw the consequence . . . it meant submission to a people whom he did not consider his equal . . . Crazy Horse feared no man and when he did surrender, it was not from volition on his part, but because his people were tired of warfare.'

The Prophecy Fulfilled
After his surrender, Short Bull recalled Crazy Horse's words to Clark:

He said 'There is a creek over there they call Beaver Creek; there is a great big flat west of the headwaters of Beaver Creek; I want my agency put right in the middle of that flat'. He said the grass was good there for horses and game. After the agency was placed there, he would go to Washington and talk to the Great Fathers. It was the only cause of misunderstanding at that time. Crazy Horse wanted to have the agency established first, and then he would go to Washington. The officers wanted him to go to Washington first.

The difference of whether Crazy Horse should go to Washington before or after the site of the agency was settled upon brought on all the trouble, little by little.

(Short Bull)

The officers at Fort Robinson were understandably fascinated by Crazy Horse, and Red Feather recalled: 'All the white people came to see Crazy Horse and gave him presents and money. The other Indians at the agency got very jealous.' The old rivalries between the Bad Faces and the Hunkpatila resurfaced and Crazy Horse attracted an increasing number of enemies. When Crook granted him permission for a feast and a buffalo hunt, Red Cloud and Spotted Tail immediately spoke against Crazy Horse to their agents.

Then, when Crazy Horse finally decided to go to Washington, the Red Cloud Lakota whispered to him of the great danger he was in. 'Other Indians were jealous of him,' Little Killer said, 'and afraid that if he went to Washington they would make him chief of all the Indians on the reservation. These Indians came to him and told him a lot of stories. After that he would not go there.' According to Carrie Slow Bear, 'Another Indian told him they would kill him either at Fort Robinson or Washington . . . Little Big Man told him that.'

In August of 1877, Crook asked the Oglala to help him fight the Nez Perce. While his people signed up, proudly parading their new guns and

Little Big Man, who in 1875, as Crazy Horse's lieutenant, threatened to kill the Black Hills commissioners. After surrendering with Crazy Horse, he switched allegiance, and schemed to supplant the Oglala chief, pinioning Crazy Horse's arms when he was killed. Lt. Bourke said of Little Big Man: 'In appearance he was crafty, but withal a man of considerable ability and force;' however the reservation Lakota spoke of him as a trouble-maker.

43

Touch the Clouds, the dignified seven-foot tall Miniconjou warrior and chief who shared Crazy Horse's fight for the Lakota's traditional freedom. Greatly feared by his enemies, he surrendered at the Spotted Tail Agency, Camp Sheridan, at the head of a singing column of warriors, on 14 April, 1877. There, Crazy Horse sought Touch the Clouds' protection when escaping arrest on the 4th September.

horses, Crazy Horse refused. Red Feather explained: 'When he came to the agency, the soldiers had made him promise not to go on the warpath any more. They told him not to fight and then to fight.' When Clark persisted in asking him to enlist, Crazy Horse snapped, 'If the Great Father wants us to fight we will go north and fight until not a Nez Percé is left.' The translator, Frank Grouard, maliciously translated this as, 'until not a white man is left.' Then Crazy Horse, exasperated by affairs at Red Cloud Agency, threatened to take his people north again, and the white officers were thrown into panic.

Crook was summoned, arriving at the Red Cloud Agency on 2nd September 1877. Two officers, Randall and Bradley, visited Crazy Horse, giving him a knife and two cigars, and the Indians were told to move across the creek for a council with Crook. Crazy Horse refused, suspicious of his white visitors.

He thought the gift of the knife meant trouble coming. He thought they shook hands with him as if they did not mean him any good. He was afraid there would be trouble at that council.

(He Dog)

When He Dog asked if this meant that Crazy Horse would be his enemy if he moved across the creek, Crazy Horse, laughing, replied:

'I am no white man! They are the only people that make rules for other people that say, 'If you stay on one side of this line it is peace, but if you go on the other side I will kill you all. There is plenty of room; camp where you please.'

When Clark asked He Dog to persuade his friend to attend, Crazy Horse replied, 'Some people over there have said too much. I don't want to talk to them any more. No good would come of it.'

As an ambulance carried Crook and Clark to the council, Red Cloud's cousin Woman's Dress rode up. He often loafed with Long Chin and Lone Bear near Crazy Horse's lodge, blankets about their heads; and he announced that Crazy Horse meant to kill Crook.

Crook returned immediately to Fort Robinson, and the next day told the Lakota chiefs, 'that they must preserve order in their own ranks and arrest Crazy Horse'. Red Feather heard White Hat offer '$100 and a sorrel horse to any Indian who would kill Crazy Horse,' and hurried to warn the betrayed Oglala of his fate.

At 9 a.m. on 4th September, eight companies of infantry left Fort Robinson for Crazy Horse's village, Clark leading 400 warriors including Red Cloud, Little Wound, American Horse and Young Man Afraid. They reached Crazy Horse's village only to find the lodges scattered, Crazy Horse having taken his wife to Spotted Tail Agency. Clark offered $200 to the first man to catch him, and it was No Water who led the pursuit. By riding hard downhill, and walking uphill, Crazy Horse reached Spotted Tail Agency that evening, while No Water killed two horses in a vain attempt to catch him.

Crazy Horse spent the night under the protection of the seven-feet Miniconjou chief Touch The Clouds. Assured that he could eventually settle at Spotted Tail Agency, Crazy Horse left to return to Red Cloud Agency in the morning, escorted by Touch The Clouds, Agent Lee and Spotted Tail's soldiers. Lee described Crazy Horse as being like, 'a frightened, trembling wild animal brought to bay, hoping for confidence one moment and fearing treachery the next. He had been under a severe strain, and it plainly showed.'

When Crazy Horse reached White River, some 10,000 Lakota had gathered at the agency. He Dog met him, warning, 'Watch your step – you are going into a bad place.' Crook had ordered Bradley to 'capture this chief, confine him, and send him under guard to Omaha.' So, while Crazy Horse was led into the adjutant's office at Fort Robinson, Lee was told that Bradley would not see the chief, and that he must be placed in the guardhouse.

Under the charge of Captain James Kennington, Crazy Horse was led towards the prison, still believing Lee's assurances that he could speak to the commanding officer. The Indian policemen Turning Bear, Wooden Sword, Leaper and Little Big Man escorted him. Passing a soldier with a bayonetted rifle, Crazy Horse saw the tiny cell's barred windows. He

Crazy Horse boasted that he would never allow the white man's camera to 'steal his shadow'. No fully authenticated image of him exists, although several photographs have been published purporting to be him. Of these, this old tin-type is the most likely to be authentic. It originated with Ellen Howard, daughter of the scout Baptiste Garnier (Little Bat) whose wife was Crazy Horse's cousin. She claimed that Little Bat and the infamous scout Frank Grouard persuaded Crazy Horse to have the photograph taken near Fort Laramie, about 1872. It bears a fascinating resemblance to written descriptions of Crazy Horse, and was authenticated as being him by Jake Herman, Fifth Member of the Oglala Sioux Tribal Council, after consultation with the Lakota elders.

smelled its foul stench and realised for the first time that he was to be imprisoned. Drawing a knife, he reeled around, slashing Little Big Man across the forearm. Then Little Big Man grasped his old friend's arms, echoing Crazy Horse's vision. American Horse and Red Cloud screamed, 'Shoot to kill!' Kennington bellowed, 'Stab the son of a bitch!'

His arms pinioned, Crazy Horse felt the bayonet of Private William Gentles pierce his back. Then it was thrust again, through his kidneys. Falling into Little Big Man's arms, Crazy Horse whispered, 'Let me go, my friends. You have got me hurt enough.' He Dog stepped up and Crazy Horse asked, 'See where I am hurt. I can feel the blood flowing.' Then Touch The Clouds picked up the Oglala gently in his arms, and carried him in to the adjutant's office.

Worm and Touch The Clouds spent the night beside Crazy Horse, who told them, 'I am bad hurt. Tell the people it is no use to depend on me any more now.' He died early in the morning of 6th September 1877. Touch The Clouds spoke quietly: 'It is good; he has looked for death and it has come.' Only now did the Lakota realise that they had killed their great warrior and chief through their fears and jealousies. One elder said later, 'I'm not telling anyone – white or Indian – what I know about the killing of Crazy Horse. That affair was a disgrace and a dirty shame. We killed our own man.'

Crazy Horse's body was placed in a coffin and carried on a travois to be placed on a scaffold at Spotted Tail Agency. When the Lakota were moved to a new agency on the Missouri, Worm broke away from his people. Wrapping his son's bones in a buffalo robe, he placed them on a scaffold, in an unknown place near Chankpe Opi Wakpala, Wounded Knee Creek:

His father hid his body so not even my sister (Black Shawl) knew where it was buried. Before he was buried a war-eagle came to walk on the coffin every night. It did nothing, only just walked about.

(Red Feather)

Chronology of Events

1830	Indian Removal Act.	1851	Horse Creek council and treaty signing.
1831	Fort Pierre built in the Dakotas.	1854	19 AUGUST: Lieutenant Grattan's party killed.
1834	Fort Laramie established. Oglala head south.	1855	3 SEPTEMBER: Blue Water Massacre. General Harney destroys Little Thunder's camp.
1841	First large wagon-trains cross the Plains.		
	Bull Bear murdered in Old Smoke's camp.	1857	29 JULY: Colonel Sumner fights Cheyenne on Solomon River.
	AUTUMN: Curly born on Rapid Creek.		
1845	15 JUNE: Colonel Kearney meets Oglala and Brulé at Laramie.	1857	SUMMER: Bear Butte Indian council.
			Upper Platte Agency moved west of Laramie.
1849	Troops stationed at Fort Laramie.	1858	Curly kills two Arapaho and is named Crazy Horse.
	Cholera sweeps the Plains.		
1850	Smallpox sweeps the Plains.		Colorado gold-rush.

1860	Upper Platte Agency moved back east of Laramie.
1861–5	American Civil War.
1862	No Water marries Black Buffalo Woman.
1864	Sand Creek Massacre. Colonel Chivington attacks Black Kettle's Cheyenne
1865	7 JANUARY: First Julesburg Station attack.
	2 FEBRUARY: Second Julesburg Station attack.
	14 JUNE: Loafers flee en route to Fort Kearney.
	25–26 JULY: Platte Bridge Station attack.
	SUMMER: Crazy Horse is made a Shirt Wearer.
	AUGUST: Powder River expeditions under General Connor and Colonels Cole and Walker.
1866	JUNE: Carrington meets Red Cloud at Laramie.
	AUGUST: Forts Reno, Phil Kearny and C.F. Smith established on Bozeman Trail.
	21 DECEMBER: The Battle of the Hundred Slain (Fetterman Massacre).
1867	23 JANUARY: Carrington relieved of command at Fort Phil Kearny.
	1 August: Hayfield Fight.
	2 AUGUST: Wagon Box Fight.
1868	JULY: Forts C.F. Smith and Phil Kearny abandoned.
	NOVEMBER: Red Cloud signs Laramie Treaty.
	Crazy Horse recognised as Oglala war chief.
1870	SUMMER: Crazy Horse and He Dog carry crow-lances in battle 'When they chased the Crows back to Camp.'
	No Water shoots Crazy Horse after elopement with Black Buffalo Woman.
	Little Hawk killed.
	AUTUMN: High Back Bone killed.
1871	Crazy Horse's daughter They are Afraid of Her born.
1872	SUMMER: Second Arrow Creek Fight.
1872	AUGUST: Major Baker's Northern Pacific Railroad Yellowstone survey.
1873	JUNE: Generals Stanley and Custer's Yellowstone survey.
1874	JULY: Custer's Black Hills expedition.
	Crazy Horse's daughter dies.
1875	SUMMER: The Lakota and Cheyenne hold great Sun Dance.
	SEPTEMBER: Black Hills commission fails to purchase Pa Sapa.
	6 DECEMBER: Indians ordered on to reservations.
1876	17 MARCH: Colonel Reynold's attack on He Dog's Powder River camp.
	Sitting Bull's Sun Dance.
	17 JUNE: Battle of the Rosebud.
	25 JUNE: Battle of the Greasy Grass (Little Bighorn).
	9 SEPTEMBER: Captain Mills attacks Iron Plume camp at Slim Buttes.
	25 NOVEMBER: Colonel Mackenzie attacks Dull Knife's Cheyenne.
	DECEMBER: Crazy Horse's emissaries killed at Fort Keogh by Colonel Miles' Crow scouts.
1877	8 JANUARY: Miles attacks Crazy Horse camp.
	Sword's Oglala delegation asks Crazy Horse to surrender.
	MARCH: Spotted Tail's Brulé delegation asks Crazy Horse to surrender.
	27 APRIL: Red Cloud claims honour of Crazy Horse surrender.
	6 MAY: Crazy Horse surrenders at Red Cloud Agency.
	6 SEPTEMBER: Crazy Horse killed.

Bibliography

Adams, A.B. *Sitting Bull* New English Library, 1975.

Ambrose, S.E. *Crazy Horse and Custer*, Purnell, 1975.

Bad Heart Bull, A. *A Pictographic History of the Oglala Sioux* University of Nebraska, 1967.

Bourke, J.G. *On the Border with Crook* Time Life, 1980.

Brandon, W. *American Heritage Book of Indians* American Heritage, 1982.

Brown, D. *Bury My Heart At Wounded Knee* Barrie & Jenkins/Pan, 1970.

Brown, J.E. *The Sacred Pipe* Penguin, 1971.

Finerty, J.F. *War Path and Bivouac* University of Oklahoma, 1961.

Grinnel, G.B. *The Fighting Cheyennes* University of Oklahoma, 1915.

Hinman, E.H. *Oglala Sources on the Life of Crazy Horse* Nebraska State Historical Society, 1976.

Hook, J. 'Crazy Horse' in *Military Illustrated* June/July, 1986.

Hook, J. *The American Plains Indians* Osprey, 1985.

Hyde, G.E. *Spotted Tail's Folk*, University of Oklahoma, 1961.

McCluhan, T.C. *Touch the Earth,* Sphere 1971.

Marquis, T.B. *Wooden Leg*, University of Nebraska 1931.

Powell, P.J. *People of the Sacred Mountain*, Harper & Row 1981.

Sandoz, M. *Crazy Horse*, Bison, 1961.

Swanton, J.R. *The Indian Tribes of North America*, Smithsonian Institution, 1952.

Taylor, C. *Warriors of the Plains*, Hamlyn, 1975.

Vaughn, J.W. *Indian Fights,* University of Oklahoma, 1966.

Vestal, S. *Sitting Bull*, University of Oklahoma, 1956.

Index

Page numbers in *italics* refer to illustrations.

Illustrations

Colour plates by Richard Hook
Line illustrations, maps and diagrams by Chartwell Illustrators
Photographs courtesy of: Bernisches Historisches Museum (pages 16, 20, 21 and 40); Museum of the American Indian, Heye Foundation (page 25); Nebraska State Historical Society (pages 32, 37, 38, 41, 43 and 44); Smithsonian Institution (pages 40 and 45)